INTERNATIONAL RELATIONS
THE BASICS

International Relations: the ·Basics is a concise and accessible introduction for students new to international relations and for the general reader. It offers the most up-to-date guide to the major issues and areas of debate and

- explains key issues including humanitarian intervention and economic justice
- features illustrative and familiar case studies from around the world
- examines topical debates on globalization and terrorism
- provides an overview of the discipline to situate the new reader at the heart of the study of global politics.

Covering all the basics and more, this is the ideal book for anyone who wants to understand contemporary international relations.

Peter Sutch is currently head of the Politics Department and Senior Lecturer in Political Thought and International Relations at Cardiff University. His current research is on international law and international justice.

Juanita Elias is Senior Lecturer in International Politics at the University of Adelaide, Australia. Her research interests include gender perspectives in international political economy, the politics of corporate social responsibility and the political economy of Malaysia and Southeast Asia.

ALSO AVAILABLE FROM ROUTLEDGE

INTERNATIONAL RELATIONS
THE BASICS

Peter Sutch and Juanita Elias

Routledge
Taylor & Francis Group

LONDON AND NEW YORK

First published 2007 by Routledge
2 Park Square, Milton Park, Abingdon, Oxon OX14 4RN

Simultaneously published in the USA and Canada
by Routledge
270 Madison Ave, New York, NY 10016

Reprinted 2007

Routledge is an imprint of the Taylor & Francis Group, an informa business

© 2007 Peter Sutch and Juanita Elias

Typeset in Aldus and Scala Sans by
Florence Production Ltd., Stoodleigh, Devon
Printed and bound in Great Britain by
Antony Rowe Ltd, Chippenham, Wiltshire

British Library Cataloguing in Publication Data
A catalogue record for this book is available from the British Library

Library of Congress Cataloging in Publication Data
Sutch, Peter, 1971–
    International relations: the basics/Peter Sutch and Juanita Elias
        p. cm.
    Includes bibliographical references and index.
        1. International relations.   I. Elias, Juanita.   II. Title.
    JZ1318.S875 2007
    327–dc22   2006038113

ISBN10: 0–415–31184–5 (hbk)
ISBN10: 0–415–31185–3 (pbk)
ISBN10: 0–203–96093–9 (ebk)

ISBN13: 978–0–415–31184–7 (hbk)
ISBN13: 978–0–415–31185–4 (pbk)
ISBN13: 978–0–203–96093–6 (ebk)

CONTENTS

Class: 327 SuT
Accession No: 112764
Type: 3 Weeks.

ILLUSTRATIONS

Figures

Boxes

ACKNOWLEDGEMENTS

A book like this relies on the input and patience of many colleagues and students. Our debts are suitably global and we would like to thank colleagues in the UK and Australia for the time they spent reading material and encouraging us to get on with it. In particular we would like to thank David Boucher, Peri Roberts, Bruce Haddock, Keiron Curtis, Edwin Egede, Stuart Shields, Jocelyn Mawdsley, Sophie Hague, Ian Hall and Andreas Gofas. Just as importantly we would like to thank Phil, Nicola, Victoria and Matthew for creating the space in their lives to let us write.

ACKNOWLEDGMENTS

1

THE NATURE OF INTERNATIONAL RELATIONS

THE BASIC VOCABULARY OF IR

The purpose of this book is to offer you a critical introduction to the basics of international relations (IR). The key word here is 'critical' rather than 'basics'. If, at the end of this introduction, you understand why the word critical is key, you will be in a strong position to move on to the next chapters. To help you reach this initial goal this introductory chapter will focus on the nature of the study of IR as an academic discipline. Here we aim to give you a sense of the 'shape' of the subject and an insight in to the challenges that lie ahead.

IR is usually characterized as a separate and discrete academic discipline. You will find separate departments of 'International Relations' or 'International Politics' in many universities. You will find separate curricula and degree schemes, and professors and lecturers of IR. However, in an important sense this separateness is artificial. On the one hand it seems intuitively simple to say that IR is a distinct entity. It is at the most basic level, the study of something that exists out there. *Inter – National – Relations*, the study of relations between nations. When we say 'nations' here we usually intend to refer to the interactions of nation-states – sovereign, territorially bounded political units like the United States of America or France. However, it is also clear that this does not tell us very much about our subject. Taking a brief glance at the world around us we find that some of the principal actors in world politics, the agents of international relations that make up the political landscape of our subject area, are not nations at all. When we look at the world of global politics we inevitably see *international* or *trans*-national governmental organizations (IGOs) such as the United Nations (UN) or the International Monetary Fund (IMF). We see regional organizations, such as the European Union (EU) or the Association of South East Asian Nations (ASEAN), important non-governmental organizations (NGOs) such as the Red Cross (and Red Crescent) or Amnesty International, and powerful multinational corporations (MNCs) with bigger annual turnovers than the gross national product (GNP) of many countries. We also find that many issues that we associate with IR transcend this basic description. Are our concerns about an HIV/AIDS epidemic in Africa, or human rights reducible to IR in this narrow sense? There is clearly much more to IR than inter-national relations.

We also find that the questions and issues that arise as an obvious part of IR seem more properly to be thought of as questions of politics, economics, law, development studies, geography, history, moral philosophy, strategic or war studies (the list could go on and on). Take a closer look at your faculty list and you will find that each 'IR specialist' is in fact a specialist in a subfield of IR. They may be experts in 'theory', 'security studies', 'international political economy', 'foreign policy studies', 'international history' or 'international law' (again the list could go on). What does all this tell us about IR? First and foremost it tells us that IR is a general descriptor for a complex, multidisciplinary subject area. To study IR is to become a generalist. It is to find a way of engaging with a hugely complex, but fascinating and politically urgent, aspect of our lives. Politics and IR share this multidisciplinarity. Those aspects of our world that we describe as political form the framework within which we live. International politics impacts on you from the price you pay for your shopping, to the laws your government is allowed to impose. It encompasses the management of the long-term ecological, political and financial effects of the world economy and the short-term effects of poverty, starvation and disease. It confronts the refugee crises that follow natural and human-made disaster, manages the conduct of war, and attempts to coordinate the prosecution of international law. If you switch on the television or pick up a newspaper, you will see international politics everywhere.

The way to begin to get a grip on this wide-ranging and challenging subject is not to become an expert in every aspect of world politics. This might be an ideal solution but it is simply not a realistic goal. Rather, you need to find a way to 'cope' with complexity and multidisciplinarity. This is what IR, as an academic discipline, and you, as a student of IR, must try to achieve. IR, at its most basic level, is a matter of orientation. It attempts to manage the deeply complex nature of world politics by breaking it down in to understandable chunks and helpful general theories. The key is to find ways of describing and analysing world politics that can both acknowledge the vast array of causal and determining factors yet give us the critical leverage we need. We need to be able to see the 'shape' of the subject to enable us to understand the general principles that inform the technicalities of international economics, law and politics. This is not to suggest that IR is in any way a second order discipline. Indeed, if you want to understand the world economy or public international law then a study of the general nature of IR is essential. IR is the background upon which the many dramas of world politics are played out. Neither is it to suggest that IR is not complex in itself. You will need to master a whole range of historical and conceptual skills. Learning to understand the historical development of 'the state', 'the international system', 'a globalized economy' etc. offers huge insights in to the nature of IR. Similarly, learning to understand the political, cultural and moral arguments that defend or criticize these features of our world is crucial to a basic understanding of IR.

One way to approach such complexity is to think about the many different professional and technical vocabularies that people use to describe world affairs. As you progress through your study of IR, it is very likely that you will be offered specialist courses or modules on international law, political economy, moral philosophy or ethics, comparative political science, security studies and so on. Each of these areas has its own technical vocabulary. The challenges you will face are many. You will need to become familiar with the formal sources of international law and its instruments. You may also be asked to consider how we go about making and justifying moral claims (such as 'it is wrong to target civilians in time of war', or 'we have a duty to eradicate poverty in the developing world') in the face of claims to the contrary. You may be required to study the macroeconomic theory of globalized markets. These steps in your bid to understand IR will be difficult but very rewarding. However, almost all students of IR begin with an introduction to the basic vocabulary of the discipline in general. This is often called IR theory. IR theory is basic to the study of world politics in that it represents a series of attempts to explain or understand the world in ways that frame the debates in foreign policy, law, ethics, security studies etc. In other words IR theory attempts to elaborate general principles that can help orientate us in our encounter with the complexities of world politics.

The need for a general viewpoint has, to a large degree, influenced the development of IR as an academic discipline. Most importantly it means that IR does not aim at a full or complete description of world politics. This would simply replicate the enormous complexity that we are trying to understand. Instead every aspect of IR focuses on key issues and ideas, highlighting them as worthy of attention because of their explanatory or critical force. Some arguments highlight specific characteristics of international politics. One example of this would be the way in which many IR scholars have sought to highlight the existence of the sovereign nation-state as the key actor in world politics. The fact that nation-states are sovereign means that they are (to a large extent) legally and politically independent. This 'fact' has been used repeatedly to explain the distinctive character of IR. It is said to explain why international law is less authoritative and effective than domestic legal systems. It is said to explain the continued occurrence of war and our inability to manage a globalized market. It is also (on a more positive note) seen as the concrete basis of our freedom, the political protection of our way of life against the backdrop of social and cultural pluralism. For all of these reasons many scholars have argued that IR should confine itself to the study of the character and actions of nation-states (what is sometimes called high-politics). It is, they argue, the key feature of IR and what makes world politics distinctive. We will return to this idea a little later. Other arguments highlight different (and sometimes contradictory) points about what they take to be the core features of world politics. Some focus on the core values that underpin human rights to make claims about the world. Others examine the nature of global interdependence, while others focus on the uneven impact the development of an international system has had on the ability of some to act effectively on the world stage and to manage their domestic affairs.

It is important to realize that different people highlight different aspects of IR for different reasons. Some are seeking a value-free description of the key features of world politics. Others are trying to make a moral or political point. There is just as much disagreement about what (if anything) counts as a value-free description as there is about what should be viewed as the most important features of IR. There is even more disagreement about what we, in ethical and political terms, *should* think of as our priorities in world politics (should we concentrate on alleviating poverty in the developing world or on developing our own resource base and security?). You need to be in a position to evaluate these claims and this book is designed to help you. Studying world politics is not so much about learning the basics of IR. It is more a question of putting yourself in a position to make informed and critical *judgements* about IR. In politics people, quite reasonably, have different opinions and priorities. This is reflected in the literature that you will engage with as you continue your studies. Ultimately your goal is to make your own decisions about the best way to understand IR or the most important issues to address. In order to achieve this you need a balanced and critical view of the options. *International Relations: The Basics* is designed to help you in your first engagement with these issues and others that form the core of IR as it is taught in universities.

THE TRADITIONAL SUBJECT MATTER OF IR

The first part of this book is designed to introduce you to what is often thought of as the traditional subject matter of IR. Here, in the first three chapters, we focus on the emergence and development of international politics in the modern period. Modern, in the context of politics and IR, means (roughly) the seventeenth century onwards.

Modernity (for IR) is the period associated with the development of the territorial, sovereign state. This vital feature of our political landscape is traditionally dated from 1648 and the 'Peace of Westphalia', the collective term for the peace treaties that drew an end to the Thirty Years War in Europe and heralded the formal beginning of the modern European states system. In the 350 years since the Peace of Westphalia much has happened. The progressive secularization of world politics, the development of the principles and instruments of international law, and the generation of international governmental organizations, from the ad hoc Congress of Vienna (1815), to the League of Nations (1919) and the UN (1945), are all important aspects of the modern period. But the way in which the territorial state (later the nation-state) took hold and spread across the whole planet is often thought of as the defining feature of IR. In Chapter 2 we will present you with a basic introduction to the history of IR. History is not a simple retelling of the past. In seeking to explain for us the most important features of 350 years of world politics, many historians and political scientists have made choices about which aspects of history are the most notable. Usually their choices are informed by their judgement about which aspects of the history of IR offer the most to us in terms of their general explanatory force. In the case of the history of IR presented in Chapter 2, we find that the role of the sovereign state in modern world politics is presented as being the feature of IR that helps us make sense of many other key features (the anarchical condition of world politics and therefore war, the nature of international law, the balance of power system). Chapter 2 will, therefore, offer a basic introduction to the rise of the modern state system ending with the demise of the League of Nations in the run-up to the Second World War.

We end our initial look at the history of international politics here to pause and reflect on the nature of IR. We will return to the history of IR in Chapters 5 and 7 when we consider the development of non-state actors in world politics and the question of whether globalization has fundamentally changed the character of world politics. However, if you are to get yourself into a position from where you can make your own informed judgements about the nature of IR you need to adopt a critical attitude to your subject immediately.

What happens to the way we understand IR if we place all of our emphasis on the central role of the sovereign state in world politics? How should we go about studying the role of the state? Do we need to look elsewhere in order to understand world politics and if so at what? What policy suggestions or general trends emerge when we emphasize one aspect of IR over another? What, when you get right down to it, is the best way to study IR?

To put it in very simple terms, those who wrote the history of IR made a judgement about its most important features. They may have done so because their interpretation of the evidence drew them that way. On the other hand they may have done so because they had a particular moral or political viewpoint. On a more technical level they may have been using academic tools (a specific understanding of the most appropriate scientific or historical method, or a view on what counts as knowledge) that may be contestable. The judgements that we will examine have informed history and policy and so they need to be treated with respect. But understanding the history of IR is a more complex exercise than you might have first imagined. Indeed our discipline is characterized by a series of debates about what the most important features of world politics are and how to study them.

ESTABLISHED DEBATES IN IR

First, let us get back to basics. Debates of this kind are a formal part of the basic vocabulary of IR. Indeed the discipline is often characterized in terms of a series of 'great debates' (see Box 1.1). Almost everything you will ever read in IR literature characterizes its position in relation to these debates. Sometimes it is in explicit allegiance to a well-defined position within these debates. More often it is in an attempt to refine one or more of the positions within a debate. Occasionally writers define their position by rejecting wholesale either one tradition in a debate or the whole idea that there are (or were) great debates at all. A broad, yet critical, understanding of this vocabulary is therefore basic to the study of IR. In what follows we will introduce you to some of the key terms of debate and introduce a few of their key features.

BOX 1.1 THE GREAT DEBATES IN IR

Realism versus idealism	1930s
Traditionalism versus behaviourism	1960s
Neo-realism versus neo-liberalism	1980s
Rationalism versus reflectivism	1990s

REALISM VERSUS IDEALISM

These 'great debates' are really about what the study of IR is or should be. The first 'great debate', and the one that reverberates throughout the discipline, is presented as realism versus idealism. Few deny that the realism versus idealism debate gave IR its character. For many realism is IR. Realism, as the term is used in IR, arose in the late 1930s and early 1940s largely in response to what was perceived as the naive thinking of liberal politicians and scholars. Realism was, argued one of its founding architects, the beginning of a political science of international relations and a necessary response to the utopianism, or wishful thinking, which characterized the study and practice of international politics between the wars. What was being attacked was the idealism or utopianism of those who believed that it was possible to build an international political system that removed conflict and competition between states, banished war as a tool of foreign policy and established 'perpetual peace'. On what scientific basis, asked the realists, did the architects of the League of Nations base their liberal idealism? The key message was very clear. You cannot wish war away. The desire to end war is all well and good but the science of international politics must proceed by placing objective analysis ahead of utopianism. The failure to do so led to the collapse of the League of Nations and ultimately to the Second World War. It is true that realism can lead to hard-headed cynicism that emphasizes the 'irresistible strength of the existing forces and the inevitable character of existing tendencies' (Carr 1939: 11). But the price of not taking a realist attitude was and is too great.

The . . . science of international politics . . . took its rise from a great
and disastrous war. The passionate desire to prevent war determined
the whole initial course and direction of the study. Like other infant
sciences, the science of international politics has been markedly and
frankly utopian.

(Carr 1939: 8)

Carr thought that a mature political science of world politics would
combine what he called purposive thinking (the desire to end war
for example) with realism. Realism however would drive the agenda
– practice must create theory rather than theory creating practice as
the failed League of Nations with its spurious belief in the harmony
of interests had allowed it to (Carr 1939: 64, 80). Carr could have
had no idea of the impact his work was to have on the nature of IR.
From the end of the Second World War until 1970 90 per cent of
data-based studies of international politics were based on realist
theoretical assumptions (Vasquez 1983). As we write this chapter
this great debate rages on. Fittingly enough, John J. Mearsheimer,
the great American realist, took the opportunity when giving the
2005 E.H. Carr memorial lecture to roundly criticize the British IR
establishment for being overrun with 'idealists who pay little
attention to power', an argument that produced a spirited response
(Mearsheimer 2005; Mearsheimer *et al.* 2005). One of the first things
you need as you embark on the study of world politics, therefore,
is a grasp of the realist approach to IR. What are the objective laws
about world politics that Realists believe we can discover? How
do they govern international politics? How should we act once we
have grounded our policy options in a proper science of international
politics? As we come to consider these questions we will explore
some of the dominant ideas in IR. Among them are discipline shaping
claims by key figures in the history of IR, such as Hans J. Morgenthau
and Kenneth Waltz, who unequivocally associated the study of IR
with the study of state power (see Box 1.2).

These thoughts are explored in some detail in Chapter 3, which
will guide you through an initial engagement with this important
tradition in its principal guises.

BOX 1.2 MORGENTHAU AND WALTZ ON IR

Politics, like society in general, is governed by objective laws that have their roots in human nature.

The main signpost that helps political realism ... is the concept of interest defined in terms of power.

Hans Morgenthau, *Politics among Nations* (1985: 4, 5)

The factors that distinguish international politics ... are: (1) that the stakes of the game are considered to be of unusual importance and (2) that in international politics the use of force is not excluded as a means of influencing the outcome. The cardinal rule of the game is often taken to be: Do what you must in order to win it.

Kenneth Waltz, *Man, The State and War* (1959: 205)

TRADITIONALISM VERSUS BEHAVIOURALISM

Realism has influenced IR to such an extent that it really drives the other established debates. The traditionalist versus behaviouralist debate is really a debate over how best to engage in a realist science of international politics. This debate pitted traditional realists (such as Morgenthau) who found the motor of power politics in IR in human nature against positivist social scientists who attempted to apply the methodology of the natural sciences to IR. The traditional realists had argued for greater objectivity in IR. The behaviouralists claimed to offer just that. A positivist approach to science insists that we rely only on observable data because, it is argued, only observable data can be verified. Realist social scientists were to have an extraordinary influence over American IR. These neo-realists focus, in a variety of ways, on the structural causes of conflict in IR (Waltz 1979; Mearsheimer 2001) or offer empirical research in to the nature of power politics that offers predictions about how states will act given the inherently anarchical condition of world affairs. 'The structure of the international system forces states which seek only to be secure nonetheless to act aggressively toward each other' (Mearsheimer 2001: 3).

Neo-realism came to dominate the discipline, almost unchallenged, particularly in the USA, until the end of the Cold War. The core arguments that support the claim that it is possible to have a realist science of IR are explored in Chapter 3.

NEO-REALISM VERSUS NEO-LIBERALISM

The success of behaviouralism, in turn, sets the scene for the next debate, the neo-realism versus neo-liberalism debate that has dominated mainstream US IR scholarship since the 1980s. We will be referring to this neo-liberal tradition as neo-liberal institutionalism in this book. The reason for this is to avoid confusion with another 'neo-liberalism', that of neo-liberal economic theory – a tradition that is also discussed in this book. You may also find that other terms are used to describe the neo-liberal institutionalist position such as 'regime theory' and 'complex interdependency'. Neo-liberal institutionalists such as Robert Keohane accepted the scientific project (the epistemology or the theory of what counts as knowledge and the methodology or how we should 'do' IR) of the neo-realists. Nevertheless they argued that the neo-realists had underestimated the importance of transnational relations (Nye and Keohane 1971). How, asked the neo-liberals, does the reality of (for example) the global economy, thought of as a context in which states interact, effect the way that states will act?

The success of neo-liberalism cannot be underestimated. Indeed in an article that explicitly builds upon the work of Vasquez that showed how influential realism was in IR from 1945 to 1970, Walker and Morton show that from 1995 to 2000 'Liberalism surpassed Realism as the leading guide to inquiry' (Walker and Morton 2005: 341). Some have gone as far to suggest that the fact the neo-realism and neo-liberalism share the scientific, methodological and epistemological approach to IR means that this debate is not really a debate as such, or at the very best it is an intra-paradigm rather than an inter-paradigm debate (Waever 1996: 149–181). This may be the case but academically these positions dominate mainstream IR and have two clear voices in policy debates concerning security and international political economy. In Chapter 4 we explore the ways in which liberalism has offered an alternative to realist approaches to IR.

Although denounced as utopianism by Carr, liberalism has a long history and broad range of different methods. While neo-liberalism is beyond doubt the dominant form of liberalism in mainstream IR there has been a resurgence of interest in normative or cosmopolitan liberalism with its emphasis on human rights, economic justice and democratisation. Setting out the basics of liberal IR theory allows you to do something that is essential to a balanced approach to your subject. It allows you to examine the basic assumptions and arguments of liberalism, in all its guises, without merely accepting Carr's assessment of the political traditions.

RATIONALISM VERSUS REFLECTIVISM

More recently however there has been a resurgence of schools of thought who are critical of positivist orthodoxy in IR (the whole idea that IR can or should be a science). Despite the dominance of what Waever (1996) calls the Neo-Neo synthesis there are many approaches to IR that stand against the realist position and that of the neo-liberals and not all of them can be usefully lumped in with the 'utopians' or 'idealists' that were the target of Carr's agenda-setting critique. Importantly a considerable amount of work has been done to show that the realist–idealist debate that is so foundational in IR scholarship is itself something of a myth (Smith 1995, 1996, 2000; Schmidt 1998; Waever 1998, 2004; Wilson 1998; Weber 2001; Quirk and Vigneswaran 2005). There never really was one single 'utopian' approach to IR and as the discipline progressed the only thing that united those on the idealist side of the debate was a rejection of some of the key arguments of those who had been setting the agenda in the study of IR. Nevertheless this founding myth is an essential part of the vocabulary of IR and if it does not reflect historical reality it has become such a commonplace in the study of IR that you must become familiar both with its basic shape and its nuances.

The debates between the neo-realist and neo-liberals, and between both of these traditions of IR and those that come under the rather catch-all title 'reflectivists' (Keohane 1989b; Smith 2000) are the real heart of IR today. Indeed Chapter 5 onwards focus in some detail on the basic issues between them. Armed with a basic, yet critical, understanding of your discipline the aim of the latter part of this book is to place you at the centre of the debates that focus on key issues in contemporary world politics including those that rage over questions of economic and political globalization and humanitarian intervention.

A MULTIPLICITY OF ACTORS

Chapter 5 explores the nature of interdependence in contemporary IR. In one sense it is beyond doubt that the stage of world politics supports a huge variety of non-state actors. The question that drives much of contemporary IR is whether or not this alters the basic nature of world politics. How far (if at all) should the realist image of an anarchical system where states are the only important actors be challenged? Should we turn instead to focus on the successes of international organizations such as the UN or regional organizations like the EU? Should security analysts focus primarily on international terrorist organizations such as al-Qaeda and collective security responses to humanitarian crises or on national military might? To what extent should IR continue to focus on state action or should we concentrate more on understandings of multilevel governance? The first step answering these questions is to become familiar with the key actors in world politics and to this end Chapter 5 explores the basics of international organizations and regional organizations, multilateralism and global governance.

BEYOND POSITIVISM IN IR

In Chapter 6 we begin to explore the reflectivist or post-positivist approaches to contemporary IR. These approaches to IR are united in a refusal to accept the traditional view about what the proper subject matter of IR is and therefore a rejection of the mainstream view about how best to study world politics. They are, however, hugely divided on the question of what we should be examining. Essentially then the rationalist versus reflectivist debate is a debate between mainstream IR and its critics. Ultimately it will be up to you to decide how best to study IR, even what to study as IR. But reaching the point where you can make an informed and critical decision is, in essence, the purpose of this book.

In very general terms these critical theories argue that the study of IR has been conducted in unduly restrictive terms. The claim is that the academic tools used to order the study of IR illegitimately ruled out, or ignored, evidence and arguments that *should* have had a huge impact on the development of world politics. The claims often go further, arguing that the way the academy limited the scope of IR has impacted, and continues to impact, drastically on the practice of world politics. Grouped together, these approaches are often called 'post-positivist' approaches, or 'reflectivist' approaches. The question that the post-positivist asks is 'why is the scientific approach applicable to IR?' In a contribution to one of the best books on the subject of post-positivism Smith explains what is at stake.

> Theories do not simply explain or predict, they tell us what possibilities exist for human action and intervention; they define not merely our explanatory possibilities but also our ethical and practical horizons.
>
> (Smith 1996: 13)

Mainstream IR theory took a very clear view on what could count as knowledge about IR – the 'truth' about world politics – when it set up the 'scientific' parameters of the discipline. In fact, argue the reflectivists, the positivists in a kind of intellectual gatekeeping act, simply stipulated what could count as facts in IR and thereby excluded forms of knowledge that did not confirm to positivism. Because of the immense success of positivism IR, Smith argued elsewhere, went on a 'forty year detour' (Smith 1992) in which it had completely avoided the normative implications of its field. The rush by feminists, critical theorists, social constructivists, postmodernists, normative political theorists and so on to remedy this has reinvigorated the discipline. One of the reiterated themes of the post-positivist IR scholars is the possibility and desirability of thinking 'beyond' the Westphalian model of IR. On the post-positivist agenda are issues such as poverty, disease, migration, religious and cultural pluralism, gender issues, environmentalism, human rights and humanitarian intervention. The sovereign state may not be a very useful tool for dealing with these issues. Let us not forget (as we point out in Chapter 2) that the sovereign state was designed to cope with the political agenda of seventeenth century Europe. Is it still the best tool we have? A common claim is that the positivist view of what counted as legitimate knowledge in IR actually hid many of these key issues from the view of analysts and politicians thus contributing to the very problems that IR should address. One influential approach to this issue is highly critical of the stucturalist claims of the neo-realists arguing that their narrow view of what counted as knowledge in IR obscured the fact that agents (people and states) also play a role in world politics – they are not merely forced to act in certain ways by the structure of international politics – the agents and structures of world affairs are mutually constituted (Wendt 1987: 350). 'Self-help and power politics are institutions, not essential features of anarchy. *Anarchy is what states make of it*' (Wendt 1992: 395, original emphasis).

While Wendt's social constructivism offers one of the least radical theoretical alternatives to mainstream IR it is critical in that it argues that we must be able to study ideas and what we call 'norms' as important factors in global politics. Norms, in essence, are established ways of doing things in international politics – but beyond that simple definition it is very difficult to pin down what a norm is. Can we do justice to the study of norms by using an approach modelled on the natural sciences? If not how do we set a research agenda in IR and what implications does it have for our grasp of how the world works? If we start to think about what norms and ideas in IR matter, then how do we decide which norms and ideas are the most important ones to focus on? Here again you will need to make some complex decisions about what IR should study and how it should go about doing so. You will need to engage with questions of epistemology (what can we *know* and how do we come to know it), of ethics (what is right and wrong, or just and unjust), of culture and politics.

GLOBALIZATION

It is not only the disciplinary horizons of IR that have expanded considerably. World politics, it is claimed, is undergoing a series of transformations. In Chapter 7 we begin to examine the apparent globalization of IR. For some analysts globalization is taking us beyond inter-national politics, although few are rash enough to write off the sovereign nation-state just yet. Globalization is something of a catch-all term that is intended to describe the ever-increasing interdependence and interconnectedness of individuals, economies and states. If globalization is a new phenomenon (and there is some dispute about this) then it is driven principally by the rapid development of the world economy, initially after the Second World War and again after the Cold War. Since 1945 we have seen the rise of international institutions such as the World Bank, the International Monetary Fund and the General Agreement on Tariffs and Trade (GATT) which became, much later and after a painful journey, the World Trade Organization (WTO). Just as importantly, however, huge transnational corporations (TNCs), exploiting new communications networks and beyond the control of national economies, grew so quickly that earlier ideas concerning international economic management had to be rethought. In an important sense economic globalization outstripped political globalization but the challenges of governance and security in the late twentieth century and at the beginning of the twenty-first century have had a remarkable impact on the shape of IR. Organizations such as the United Nations or the European Union are the clearest example here, but there are now more than 400 international governmental organizations that exist (often uneasily) side by side with states. There are even more international non-governmental organizations (INGOs), tens of thousands of lobby groups, charities, professional associations working effectively at a global level. Economic policy, legal principles and political goals are discussed, decided and often policed at a transnational level. Security is also a global issue. The deployment of military force is often coordinated through the UN or North Atlantic Treaty Organization (NATO). Weapons of mass destruction make the global impact of war a terrifying reality, and we face new threats from international terrorist organizations that have changed the way that some of the most powerful nations on earth think about security. While globalization is driven principally by economic factors, it is clearly also a series of political, legal, social, and cultural developments. These developments are not always positive. What, for some, is the triumph of global capitalism impacts on the world unevenly. The gap between rich and poor has widened creating a political and economic deficit between the global 'north', the rich developed nations, and the global 'south' the developing nations. For many, globalization offers the prospect of American dominance and cultural homogenization, dependence not interdependence. Globalization impacts on the individual too. We are now connected, morally and causally, through our participation in global economic and political frameworks, to distant strangers who we may never meet and as yet unborn generations who will feel the impact of our custodianship of the environment. In charting the principal features of globalization you will be asked to consider how, if at all, globalization changes the priorities of IR.

THE CHALLENGES OF GLOBALIZATION

The challenges of globalization are many. In our final chapter you will be asked to explore the implications of these recent trends in IR. In part this depends on a good understanding of the nature of globalization. What exactly do all these factors add up to? Are we transcending the Westphalian system? If so is it a truly globalizing experience or is it simply another case of the rich and powerful ganging up on the poor and vulnerable, imperialism and exploitation by the back door? To explore the tensions at the very heart of contemporary international politics we invite you to consider the basics of two key issues. The first is the vexed but urgent issue of humanitarian intervention. Bit by bit the international community has come to view the use of force in world affairs as a tool to provide humanitarian assistance to the most vulnerable in the world, those suffering ethnic cleansing, genocide or war crimes. But the idea of humanitarian intervention sits uneasily with a system of international politics that rests on the sovereignty of state actors. How should we rethink IR in a world where humanitarian intervention is both a right and an obligation? The second key issue is no less urgent. The plight of the millions of impoverished peoples is well known to most and the peoples of the UN have come together remarkably to try and do something positive about it. In exploring the elaboration of and progress towards achieving the UN's millennium development goals we explore questions of global economic justice. Can we say that we have a duty of justice to prevent the suffering of the worlds poor? What is preventing us from delivering on our promises to help? In introducing you to these key issues we intend to place you, fully equipped with an understanding of the principal debates that IR has at the heart of contemporary political issues that constitute our shared world.

CONCLUSION

We have covered a lot of ground in this first chapter but it is intended to give you an overview of the challenges that lie ahead and to preface a more systematic engagement with the basics of IR that follow in the next chapters. The issues and questions that we have looked at in outline here, and more, are at the forefront of contemporary politics. We cannot help but be interested in them. Studying the basics of IR will put you in a position to make an informed judgement about these vital issues. But you should note, once again, that *you* will have to make a judgement. You cannot simply learn the right answers, or the correct opinions. It is not that sort of subject. Coming to understand the basics of IR allows you to get a sense of the context in which such judgements are to be made and to begin to see what have been considered as the limitations and possibilities for political action. A critical understanding of the historical developments of IR is essential here. More than this, an engagement with the basics of IR will allow you to learn about, and hone, the critical skills that you need in order to make judgements about the world. IR is not just the empirical (scientific or factual) study of world politics. But even this aspect of your task is fraught with hidden dangers. You need to learn about the possibilities and pitfalls of discovering 'what is out there'. What counts as knowledge? What assumptions are you bringing to your study of IR? Reading the history of IR, whether you are looking at the institutional development of world politics, the nature of international law, or policy-making, situates you deep in these debates. Your judgements here will colour your view of IR and so you need to be aware that you are taking a particular stand. Another basic aspect of IR is the tendency (perhaps the desirability) of making normative judgements. Politics is a normative subject in that people hold, and advocate, contestable moral and social positions. It has been claimed, by different people at different times and for different reasons, that (for example) only fellow citizens count (and that foreigners can be killed or enslaved, or are worth less morally) or, conversely, that we have a moral and political duty to those dying of poverty related causes the world over. These arguments do not fall naturally from a 'factual' study of the development of IR and so we need to learn the language of moral and political argument. What we are talking about here is the need to grasp the foundations of IR. Foundationalism is a technical term that it is worth learning early. It is a term that describes the underlying arguments that inform opinions and judgements about the world. It also describes for us the place we need to look if we are to gain critical purchase on the huge range of different claims that people make about IR.

This book is designed to help ease you in to the study of IR. The subject is intrinsically fascinating, often horrifying, intellectually challenging, and political urgent. It offers you the opportunity to enter the debates that inform our lives and the lives of everyone across the globe. On that note we must turn immediately to our task.

TOPICS FOR DISCUSSION

1 What does a critical engagement with IR entail?
2 In what sense is IR theory basic to the study of world politics?
3 What are the great debates in IR?
4 What do you think might be the benefits or difficulties of having a science of IR?
5 What is significant about post-positivist or reflectivist approaches to contemporary IR.

FURTHER READING

This book is designed as a first step in the study of IR rather than as a comprehensive textbook. As a discipline IR benefits from a wealth of very good textbooks. Some offer detailed introductions to key aspects of IR such as the historical development of the international political system, or globalization, or IR theory etc. Others focus more specifically on key sub-disciplines such as foreign policy, conflict resolution or international law. Others focus more narrowly still, taking one vital institutional feature (the United Nations, the state), or policy area (human rights), or theory (realism) as their subject matter. These books, some of which will be listed in later chapters where their relevance is most obvious, are the next essential step.

GENERAL INTRODUCTIONS

Brown, C. (2001) *Understanding International Relations,* second edition, Basingstoke: Palgrave.

Jackson, R. and Sørensen, G. (2003), *Introduction to International Relations: Theories and Approaches,* second edition, Oxford: Oxford University Press.

TRADITIONAL IR THEORY

Burchill, S. and Linklater, A. *et al.* (2005) *Theories of International Relations,* third edition, Basingstoke: Palgrave Macmillan.

Wight, M. (1991) *International Theory: The Three Traditions,* ed. G. Wight and B. Porter, Leicester, Leicester University Press.

GLOBALIZATION

Baylis, J. and Smith, S. (eds) (2001) *The Globalisation of World Politics: An introduction to International Relations,* second edition, Oxford: Oxford University Press.

Held, D. and McGrew, A. (eds) (2003) *The Global Transformations Reader: An Introduction to the Globalization Debate,* second edition, Cambridge: Polity Press.

INTERNATIONAL LAW

Evans, M. (ed.) (2003) *International Law,* Oxford: Oxford University Press.

CRITICAL APPROACHES

Smith, S., Booth, K. and Zalewski, M. (eds) (1996) *International Theory: Positivism and Beyond,* Cambridge: Cambridge University Press.

Weber, C. (2001) *International Relations Theory: A Critical Introduction,* London: Routledge.

NORMATIVE APPROACHES

Brown, C. (2002) *Sovereignty, Rights and Justice: International Political Theory Today,* Cambridge: Polity Press.

Boucher, D. (1998) *Political Theories of International Relations from Thucydides to the Present,* Oxford: Oxford University Press.

ANARCHY AND THE ORIGIN OF THE MODERN INTERNATIONAL SYSTEM

World politics 1648–1939

In our introductory chapter we suggested that modern international relations took their principal characteristics from the peace settlements that drew the Thirty Years War to a close in 1648. In this chapter we explore this claim in order to generate a basic introduction to some of the core features of international politics. We cannot offer a comprehensive history of modern international relations here but we can sketch a history of the rise and rise of a system of interaction between sovereign states that came to be the defining feature of global politics. The aim of IR scholars has been to derive from the history of world politics models of political interaction that can allow us to gain some critical purchase on the subject, or that can allow us to generalize about the nature of international relations. Because this is the principal aim of the student of IR detailed historical accounts of the period in question are often sacrificed in favour of an historical narrative that places heavy emphasis on key features of that history that are said to provide us with insights into the general character of international society in the modern period. It is the case that there is some disagreement about what the key features of modern IR are, or how best to understand them. Nevertheless there is a basic history of IR that you need to be familiar with even if you must treat it critically.

THE MAKING OF MODERNITY

Politics, with and between groups, has taken a variety of forms. We could learn much from an extended examination of the interplay between the *Poleis* (city-states) of the ancient Greek world, or the empire building of the Romans. However, if we are to examine the historical development of the modern system of international politics we need to examine europe in the centuries before and after the Peace of Westphalia.

THE SOVEREIGN STATE IN MODERN INTERNATIONAL POLITICS

The reason for this can be reduced to the historical development of one characteristically modern phenomenon – the sovereign state. The sovereign state is the principal actor in modern international relations (just as the *Polis* or city state was the main actor in the ancient Greek world). The sovereign state is a geo-political reality and a legal concept. Just as importantly sovereignty is a political doctrine, perhaps the defining political doctrine of modernity. Indeed many commentators believe it to be key to understanding IR.

> The fundamental cause of war is not historic rivalries, nor unjust peace settlements, nor nationalist grievances, nor competitions in armaments, nor imperialism, nor poverty, not the economic struggle for markets and raw materials, nor the contradictions of capitalism, nor the aggressiveness of Fascism or Communism; though some of these may have occasioned particular wars. The fundamental cause is the absence of international government; in other words, the anarchy of sovereign states.
>
> (Wight 1995: 101)

The sovereign state can be defined in very loose terms as a territorially defined political society that is recognized (and recognition is a formal or legal act) as being solely responsible for the governance of that territory and, on the international stage, as independent from any political or religious superior. Sovereignty is also a political doctrine that captures the ideas of freedom, independence and self-determination that are the primary claims of existing states and the major aspiration of many subnational, cultural, ethnic and religious groups who are subsumed in the territory of existing states. Because the key actors in international politics are taken to be sovereign the pattern of relations between them is necessarily anarchical or without hierarchical political structures. Our subject then is the modern states system that began to emerge after the treaty of Westphalia and understanding its nature is our primary goal.

IR AS THE STUDY OF 'POWER POLITICS'

It is often claimed that the development of the sovereign state dictates the very structure of international politics and determines the pattern of relations that we set out to study. First, because the actors in world politics are sovereign then international relations must be anarchical. Second, the essential anarchy of a system of sovereign states led to the sincere belief that the study of IR was, at its very core, distinct from the study of domestic politics. Where domestic politics was taken to be the study of the institutions of government IR was not to become the study of the institutions of international governance but, instead, the study of power politics. In his influential work of that title Martin Wight (1995) wrote:

> It has the merit of pointing to a central truth about international relations, even if it gets certain other things out of focus. For, whatever else it may suggest, 'power politics' suggests the relationship between independent powers, and we take such a state of affairs for granted. It implies two conditions. First there are independent political units acknowledging no political superior, and claiming to be 'sovereign'; and secondly, there are continuous and organised relations between them. This is the modern states-system. We have the independent units, which we call states, nations, countries or *powers*, and we have a highly organised system of continuous relations between them, political and economic, diplomacy and commerce, now peace, now war.
>
> (Wight 1995: 23, original emphasis)

Wight is suggesting that IR is defined by several core features that characterize the modern-states system. That these features, forged in the aftermath of the Thirty Years War and refined through more than three centuries of conflict, cooperation and economic competition, can be said to be constant is something we need to explore. It is undoubtedly the case that the nature of the 'independent units' in question has changed much. Similarly the mechanisms through which sovereign independence is maintained have been refined and developed over time. Nevertheless international politics can be described as relations between independent units determined, at a fundamental level, to preserve that independence.

THE WESTPHALIAN SYSTEM OF INTERNATIONAL POLITICS

You will often find the modern international system described as the Westphalian system. This is often, although controversially, contrasted with the contemporary globalized world political system and the pre-modern period where, it is argued, the world had a very different shape. The claims, found everywhere in books and articles on the birth of the modern system of international relations at Westphalia in 1648 are not really intended as accurate historical claims. Indeed if they were they would be rejected as false. Rather, such claims are traditional shorthand for the beginning of the modern period in which key features of international politics – often ascribed to the Westphalian treaties but at best only implicit in the text of those settlements – were developed. As Osiander (2001) shows in his historical exploration of the nature of the Peace of Westphalia, the traditional account of the origins of the Westphalian system is much less but also much more than a straightforward history of the period.

> On a deeper level the conventional view may serve an important function. A typical founding myth, it offers a neat account of how the 'classical' European system, the prototype of the present international system came about. Conveniently and comprehensively it explains the origin of what are considered the main characteristics of that system such as territoriality, sovereignty, equality, and non-intervention. It fits perfectly with the accepted view of what international relations is about, or at least has 'traditionally' been about: relations of a specific kind (with the problem of war occupying a central position) among actors of a specific kind (territorial, sovereign, legally equal). While IR authors

are divided on the applicability of this conventional model to current
phenomena, very rarely do they question its applicability to the past.
(Osiander 2001: 266)

There is something hugely resonant and important about this
historical tale. But we need to be aware that it is a tale told to highlight
particular issues rather than 'The Truth'. The background to the
history of the rise of the Westphalian system is one of a competition
for a world that was developing in many new directions. The great
Christian Empire that had dominated Europe had split by 1054
between the Eastern Orthodox Church and the Western *Respublica
Christiana*. The Western Empire was, in theory at least, under the
supreme rule of the Pope. In reality princes, kings, and nobles asserted
their authority across a patchwork of royal territories and feudal
privilege. In his seminal history, *The Evolution of International
Society*, Adam Watson (1992) highlights three vital factors that forced
medieval Europe to take the turn towards modernity. The first two
factors, the Renaissance and the Reformation, were pulling away
from the idea of a universal Christian Empire and a single, western
European order. The third factor was the attempt by the Habsburgs
to sustain their empire across the whole region. This bid for massive
political power was so severely resisted by the other emerging
European powers that the anti-hegemonic character of the modern
European states system was determined (Watson 1992: 169).

The cultural and social developments we associate with the
Renaissance are far too intricate for us to deal with but for our
purposes the key movement was essentially political. In politics
the Italian Renaissance is associated with the rise of the *Stato*,
independent city-states, under the control of secular rulers concerned
with practical power politics or *ragione di stato* (more often called
raison d'état or reason of state in IR literature). Nicolò Machiavelli
(much caricatured as the demonical 'old Nic' yet celebrated as a doyen
of realist politics) captures this moment in history brilliantly in his
advice to the statesmen of the day in *The Prince*. For Machiavelli,
the *virtú* of the prince is to be a strong as lion and as cunning as
a fox, to be able to use the impression of adhering to the customary
moral norms of society but able to act ruthlessly when the
political situation demands it. This essential political skill is built

upon the ability to see politics 'realistically', the key force of politics is necessity.

> It is necessary for a Prince wishing to hold his own to know how to do wrong, and to make use of it or not according to necessity.
>
> (Machiavelli, *The Prince*, Chapter XV, 1515)

The rise of the *stato* pitched the ambitions of city-states against the universal authority of the Pope. It also pitched the practical, secular demands of politics against the religious ambitions of Rome. It bred a new kind of political leader and a new kind of politics. The idea, captured by Machiavelli, was that a political leader owed his first allegiance to the success of the state. The idea that certain forms of political action are necessary in a world of states has tremendous currency in IR often to the point where political leaders claim that foreign policy is framed in response to the dictates of the system rather than as a series of politically and morally informed choices (Raymond 1998–1999). Reason of state or practical politics called for secular and instrumental rule, a call that was to be answered in modern IR.

The second great development in this period of history was the Reformation. This was a series of religious movements as Lutheran and, a little more than half a century later, Calvinist Protestant movements revolted against the power of the Roman Catholic Church. The political impact of the Reformation was to reinforce and hasten the spread of independent states across Europe. The Habsburgs, who controlled huge tracts of European territory, were a staunchly Catholic dynasty who, despite agreeing to the Augsburg settlement of 1555 which gave every ruler the right to decide the character of religion in their own domain, successfully maintained a Catholic empire and a sustained counter-reformation in the face of constant war on one front or another. By the middle of the seventeenth century a war-weary Europe was ready for a remarkable change.

The Peace of Westphalia incorporated the treaties of Münster and Osnabrück and officially put an end to the long wars between Protestant and Catholic powers that had raged across the continent. The peace settlements effectively broke the power of the Habsburg

Holy Roman Empire, firmly established the idea of religious autonomy that had been agreed at Augsberg nearly a century before and paved the way for the institution of a system of independent states. The treaty of Münster also recognized the 300 or so small states of the Holy Roman Empire as having the right to declare and wage war or enter into alliances with foreign powers (Cassese 2001: 21). The geo-political settlements were still a far cry from the nation-state system of contemporary Europe but the principles it established provide the basis for much modern IR. These ideas are crucial to understanding not just the peace settlement at the end of the Thirty Years War but the inter-national system that they were to define for generations to come. The idea of sovereignty meant that territorial states of unequal size and power were to be considered legally equal and independent. As Vattel (1758), an eminent international lawyer, put it,

> power or weakness does not in this respect produce any difference. A dwarf is as much a man as a giant; a small republic is no less a sovereign state than the most powerful kingdom.
>
> (Vattel 1916 [1758]: 45)

The ruler was sovereign in his or her own realm in that no other ruler, religious or secular, had any authority in that domain. The treaties gave them the right to enter into alliances with foreign powers and to declare war. In essence it gave the states legal personality in international affairs. As Cassese notes,

> Only a limited number of legal persons, that is holders of international rights, powers, and obligations, make up the international community. The fundamental or primary subjects are states. They are paramount because they are the international entities which, besides controlling territory in a stable and permanent way, exercise the principal lawmaking and executive 'functions' proper of any legal order. . . . They possess the full legal capacity, that is the ability to be vested with rights, powers and obligations. Were they to disappear, the present international community would either fall apart or change radically.
>
> (Cassese 2001: 46)

THE UNIVERSALIZATION OF THE WESTPHALIAN SYSTEM

Westphalia established the sovereignty of only the small states in the heart of Europe that were named in the treaties. However, the way in which this system of international politics became a global phenomenon was extraordinary. Two key historical developments that laid the groundwork for the success of the modern state system were the decline of the Ottoman Empire and European imperialism and colonialism. After Westphalia the Ottoman Empire still controlled vast territories in south-east Europe, Asia and Africa and it was a massive European power in its own right. It was, however, very different from the other European powers and insisted on dealing with them in its own Islamic terms rather than accept the public law of Europe or the discourses of the Westphalian system. In 1683 the Ottomans besieged Vienna in a bid to conquer their old Habsburg enemy but suffered a surprising and catastrophic defeat (Quataert 2003: 2). The Ottoman Empire persisted until 1922 but it was in decline and under immense pressure to accept the European discourses of diplomacy and international law. In 1856 the Ottoman Empire's accession to the treaty that brought the Crimean War to a close and brought a temporary truce to the war in Eastern Europe gave the Ottomans a formal place in international society. Continuing Russian–Turkish conflict and the peace settlements that satisfied the great powers, the 1878 treaties of San Stefano and Berlin, meant that the Ottomans lost most of their European territories. In short the biggest non-western power that could have influenced the modern international system was forced to accept Westphalian terms.

The struggle for influence between the European powers spread well beyond the European theatre. The history of the seventeenth, eighteenth, nineteenth and twentieth centuries is a history of global expansion, conquest and colonization. European colonialism, and later anti-colonial nationalism, was to have just as far-reaching an impact on the shape of the modern international system as the wars of early modern Europe. The European powers extended their political and economic dominance into the Americas, Asia, Africa and the Pacific. Somewhat ironically perhaps the reactions to imperialism saw the consolidation of the Westphalian system. Conquered peoples and colonists seeking self-rule wanted one thing more than anything – sovereign independence. Thus the history of anti-colonialism is also a history of the universalization of the European state system (Box 2.1).

BALANCE OF POWER AND WORLD POLITICS

With the universalization of the Westphalian system and the sovereign state came the anarchical and anti-hegemonic character of the international system. To say the international system is anti-hegemonic is to say that it resists any attempt by one actor (a state, or an alliance of states) to gain power over the others. As we look over the history of international politics we see that attempts to gain an all-powerful position are not unusual. Actors have sought military or strategic advantage through alliances that intimidate others, through direct use of force and through the development of superior

BOX 2.1 JACKSON ON THE SPREAD OF THE MODERN EUROPEAN STATES SYSTEM

One of the most significant developments in the history of international politics was adoption of originally European discourses of diplomacy and international law by political authorities around the world – whether that was done reluctantly (e.g. by Japan and the Ottoman Empire in the nineteenth century who thereby renounced their self-defined status as beyond the states-system and superior to it) or enthusiastically (e.g. by Asian and African anti-colonial nationalists in the twentieth century who thereby escaped from European Imperialism and gained independence). Before the twentieth century there was no express political dialogue on a global scale, no political conversation of humankind that embraced all cultures and civilizations. The institution of such a conversation was a specific achievement of modern statecraft connected with the expansion of the society of states.

Robert Jackson, *The Global Covenant* (2000: 10)

military organization or weapons technology. They often try to forge economic alliances that give them a distinct trading advantage. It is also interesting to see how the attempt by some actors to assert religious authority, or to claim moral superiority, has had such an enormous effect on the history of world politics.

Despite the fact that international politics appears to be a history of successive bids for dominance the system continually restores the *status quo ante* or, at the very least, returns to a configuration of roughly equal and independent actors. The modern international system is characterized by attempts to maintain a balance of power. Michael Sheehan's (1996) study of this phenomenon offers the following definition.

> The phrase 'balance of power' implies a certain permanence – a 'balance' is a finished product. The reality of international relations, however, is that movement and change, not stasis are its characteristic features. . . . Power is never permanently balanced, rather the states must be permanently engaged in the act of balancing power, of adjusting and refining it in response to the perpetual ebb and flow of power within the system.
>
> (Sheehan 1996: 13)

Successive peace settlements clearly responding to this anti-hegemonic principle punctuate the history of modern international politics. Indeed, the clearest expression of a systemic drive to ensure a balance of power can be found in the treaties that followed the wars that were the forge of the European state system (see Box 2.2). Often these settlements radically altered the geo-political map of Europe. Small states were abolished, large states broken up, and territorial borders were significantly altered. Understanding the dynamic of this anti-hegemonic principle has therefore been taken to be the key to understanding the very nature of modern international politics (Morgenthau 1948; Waltz 1979). Similarly, influential figures in international law cite the balance of power system as being fundamental to the existence and operation of international law (Oppenheim 1955). There is, of course, fierce debate about how best to understand this propensity to form a balance of power. For some, the system forces states to act in their own self-interest and

BOX 2.2 PEACE TREATIES THAT SHAPED IR

Treaty of Westphalia 1648 – At the end of the Thirty Years War
Treaty of Utrecht 1713 –Wars of the Spanish Succession
Congress of Vienna 1815 – At the defeat of Napoleon I
Treaty of Versailles 1919 – The end of the First World War
UN Charter 1946 – A response to the Second World War

self-interest always lies in the construction of a balance of power (Waltz 1979: 118). A balance of power is thus a necessary characteriztic of an anarchical system. For others the degree of cooperation required to construct and maintain an effective balance of power suggests a high level of international management and interdependence (Jervis 1992). For some the many political configurations of Europe are simply different instances of the classical balance of power (see Gulick (1955) on the Concert of Europe; Carr (1939) on the League of Nations; Gross (1948) on the UN). For others key attempts at international governance go well beyond a mere balance of power politics (see Krasner (1995) on 'Compromising Westphalia'; Jervis (1992) on the Concert of Europe). The question an historian of international relations must answer is how should we characterize the international system of the Concert of Europe that stood from the end of the Napoleonic Wars to the Crimean War 1815–1854, or the League of Nations between the two world wars, or the role of the United Nations in global politics today? The question is important because not only does a grasp of the nature of the balance of power help us understand the world of international politics but also it informs policy decisions because the tools we have available to us in an anarchical political system are rather different from the tools available to us in an international society characterized by effective transnational governmental institutions.

ANARCHICAL POLITICS: WAR, DIPLOMACY AND LAW IN INTERNATIONAL RELATIONS

If the anti-hegemonic structure of modern world politics can be seen in the operation of a balance of power system of politics then we begin to gain some insight in to the key mechanisms through which sovereign states maintain this delicate balance. States interact in an anarchical system using three major tools: international law, diplomacy and war. All three of these tools are formal institutions of the international system. Each institution is, in essence, a way of dealing with conflicts of interest between sovereign states and each has developed an ever more refined system of rules relating to the management of its subject. All three institutions have a history that goes back well before the modern period. War is a seemingly permanent feature of human political history but you must not mistake war for the breakdown of politics or view it as an aberration in international relations. In the much quoted dictum of Clausewitz, 'war is the continuation of politics by other means' (Clausewitz 1968: Chapter VI). It is a rule-bound method of conflict resolution and we have long had rules about who can declare war (and under what circumstances), how we can fight it, and how to draw it to a close (Roberts and Guellf 2000: 3–4). During the modern period the development of the international system along with advances in the technology of warfare (from gunpowder to nuclear weapons) has had a significant impact on the ways in which the international community seeks to regulate war. From specific conventions banning the use of certain types of weapon (such as the Hague conventions of 1899) to more ambitious covenants and charters aiming at the rejection of war as a means of conflict resolution (the League of Nations, the United Nations) the laws of war and peace have gained a distinctly modern form. Similarly, while a recognizable system of diplomacy (including the immunity of envoys) can be seen in the dealings of the ancient Greeks, the rise of the *stato* in fifteenth century Italy saw the formation of a recognizably modern system of permanent resident diplomatic missions that was to develop through the French system in the middle of the twentieth century to the permanent diplomatic conferences of the League and the UN (Berridge 2002).The very character of war and diplomacy as tools of conflict resolution is given by the nature of the system in which they operate. The same is true of international law. International law is not the product of the legislative process of government as state law is. It aims at regulating the relations of states rather than individuals and importantly it takes account of existing power relationships (Cassese 2001: 12) and as such the sources of law are international treaties and customary state practice as well as judicial decisions, the writings of jurists, military manuals and, more recently, the resolutions of international bodies. A history of the practice of war, diplomacy and international law offers intriguing insights into the nature of modern international society and the politics of what Hedley Bull famously called the anarchical society (Bull (1995) [1977]). The key is to recognize that a grasp of the nature of the balance of power is essential to a grasp of IR. This is not just because it helps us understand how the great powers of modern Europe acted and offers insights in to the conduct of European statecraft. The modern European states system has been hugely successful and influential. What started as a political settlement to a European problem was to be exported across the globe. The Westphalian system became the universal system of international politics and, many argue, still underpins contemporary international relations.

GETTING BEYOND THE STATE?
THE LEAGUE OF NATIONS

Earlier in this chapter we argued that the student of IR had to make some decisions about how best to characterize what appear to be significant developments in political history such as the establishment and conduct of a Concert of Europe, the League of Nations, or the United Nations. There is no doubt that the level of international cooperation that we can see in the operation of the League and the UN is of real historical significance. The question is whether or not these attempts to build international organizations changed the essential nature of world politics.

Woodrow Wilson was the US President who led his nation into the First World War in 1917. In January 1918, in a speech to Congress, President Wilson famously set out 'Fourteen Points' designed to ensure that after the war,

> the world be made fit and safe to live in; and particularly that it be made safe for every peace-loving nation which, like our own, wishes to live its own life, determine its own institutions, be assured of justice

and fair dealing by the other peoples of the world as against force and selfish aggression.

(Full text of the speech can be found at
http://www.yale.edu/lawweb/avalon/wilson14.htm
on the website of the Avalon Project, Yale University)

Wilson's plan was designed to change the very constitution of world politics. His liberal internationalism wanted to move beyond the balance of power politics of anarchical international relations. He was convinced that establishing firmer institutional structures that supported an idea of collective security would highlight the fact that all peace loving nations could be seen to have a common interest in peace rather than war. His idea of a general association of nations was to find concrete (if imperfect) expression in the League of Nations established at the Paris Peace Conference of 1919.

EXPERIMENTS IN GLOBAL GOVERNANCE?
THE COVENANT OF THE LEAGUE OF NATIONS

The covenant of the League of Nations created an organization of 42 states with a bold remit to manage international affairs (Box 2.3). The structure of the organization was to set the pattern for the future of international and regional organizations and diplomacy (Armstrong *et al.* 2004: 31). It consisted of three principal organs. The council was the most important organ of the League and was in charge of security issues. While some, principally Britain, had argued that membership of the council should be open to major powers, article 4 of the covenant, provided for four non-permanent members to be elected from the assembly in addition to the permanent 'principal allied and associated powers' (the British Empire, France, Italy and Japan). Every member country was represented in the assembly which dealt with budgetary matters, elected non-permanent members to the council, amendments to the covenant and, under article 4, was to deal with 'any matter within the sphere of action of the League or affecting the peace of the world'. As such it became the body that the council reported to annually. The final organ of the League was its secretariat, a permanent body of international officials.

BOX 2.3 PREAMBLE TO THE COVENANT OF THE LEAGUE OF NATIONS

THE HIGH CONTRACTING PARTIES

In order to promote international cooperation and to achieve international peace and security

by the acceptance of obligations not to resort to war,

by the prescription of open, just and honourable relations between nations,

by the firm establishment of the understandings of international law as the actual rule of conduct among Governments, and

by the maintenance of justice and a scrupulous respect for all treaty obligations in the dealings of organized peoples with one another,

Agree to this Covenant of the League of Nations.

It was not just the edifice of the League of Nations that suggested a real change in world politics. Rather it was the role that the authors of the covenant had in mind that was groundbreaking. The preamble to the 26 articles of the covenant offered a huge amount of hope particularly in terms of the collective rejection of war and acceptance of international law. After the carnage of the First World War the desire to establish a genuine system of collective security where war between members was unthinkable (article 10) and an attack on one was to be considered an attack on all (article 16) was very understandable. But the League was more than a security actor. Its economic, legal and social agenda was equally impressive. It dealt with global problems including environmental issues, health issues and even humanitarian issues such as refugee crises and national reconstruction. It established the Permanent Court of International Justice, the Health Organization and the International Labour Organization. Yet different commentators view the League in different ways. Armstrong *et al.* argues:

> Although lacking any mechanisms to enforce observance of these
> standards, this did imply a limited right for the League to concern itself
> with human rights – a subject that was to become increasingly important
> to the League's successors. Second, the Covenant was a clear
> acknowledgment of the increasing range of common interests shared
> by states outside the field of security, and the need for more effective
> centralized supervision of these.
>
> (Armstrong *et al.* 2004: 21)

Yet Cassese believes that the 'system set up in 1919 greatly
resembles that devised in 1648' primarily because there was no real
attempt to restrict the right of sovereign nation-states to go to war
in pursuit of their interests (Cassese 2001: 32). There is no doubt
that the League paved the way for the UN. Equally, however, there
is no doubt that the League was a spectacular failure as two decades
after these bold declarations were made the world was once again
in the grip of total war.

THE COLLAPSE OF THE LEAGUE OF NATIONS

What went wrong? History tells us that the ethos of the League of
Nations was shattered by a series of serious political failures. The first
and perhaps most damaging was the failure to keep the USA on board.
The First World War had clearly marked the end of European
dominance of world politics. Therefore when the US Senate rejected
the Versailles Treaty, the League effectively lost its most important
member. One consequence of this was that the European powers
consistently failed to use the League's potential and often ignored
or made scant use of the articles that allowed for decisive action
to be taken against aggressors. This, coupled with the withdrawal
of Germany, Italy, Japan and the Soviet Union at various points,
undermined the unanimity that was supposed to underwrite the
potential of the League to act effectively as a genuine international
governmental organization in world politics. The crises came to a head
in the face of the Japanese occupation of Manchuria in 1931. This
annexation of one of China's richest provinces was part of the 'Tanaka
plan', a campaign of territorial expansion that was a response to the
view that Japan had not had its fair share of the spoils of the First

World War. The idea that moral condemnation from the League would prevent such aggression was exposed as wishful thinking. Indeed Japan, a genuinely powerful actor in its own right and a permanent member of the council, objected to criticism from the relatively powerless members of the assembly. This, coupled with the failure of the League's commitment to collective security to produce decisive action, spelled the beginning of the end for the League and the 'Utopian' experiment of liberal internationalism. When in 1935 the League failed again to respond to aggression (this time in the face of the Italian invasion of Ethiopia) the fate of the experiment was sealed.

THE REALIST CRITIQUE OF THE LEAGUE OF NATIONS

For E.H. Carr (1939), who was at the Paris negotiations in 1919, it was not Japanese or Italian aggression that sank the League and liberal hopes for peace. It was not even the failure of will that the principal members of the League clearly demonstrated. Carr's diagnosis was based on a more fundamental set of problems. For Carr the League of Nations and the liberalism that underpinned its ideals was, in his words that were to ring down the ages in IR scholarship, 'utopian'.

The charge that Carr levelled against this political experiment was that it allowed abstract rationalism, in the form of a commitment to Lockean liberalism, to inform the political response to the peace settlement. Liberalism may well be suited to the internal workings of the European nations that were themselves the product of the Enlightenment. But, as Carr notes, to transplant liberalism beyond Europe, let alone on to an international system of sovereign, yet (in terms of development and power) unequal, states was absurd. Not only did the liberal internationalists not pay attention to the realities of world politics but also they failed to understand that the dominance of their (liberal) way of thinking was itself the outcome of power politics, a product of the allied victory in the First World War. For Carr,

> The exposure of the real basis of the professedly abstract principles commonly invoked in international politics is the most damning and most convincing part of the realist indictment of utopianism.
>
> (Carr 1939: 87)

The simple fact is that the utopianism of the League of Nations liberals is shown up by the failure of the League itself. For Carr, and many others, the failure of the League was simply a failure to recognize and act upon the background conditions of international society. If world politics is anarchical then, argued Carr, the idea that we should design international institutions to respond to a real harmony of interests that underlay the obvious disharmony of national interest is absurd. A realistic way forward would be to recognise that conflicting national interests need to be recognised for what they are – a natural part of international politics. If power politics is the basis of international politics then we can expose the liberal programme of action for what it is – power politics incarnate. For Carr,

> the bankruptcy of utopianism resides not in its failure to live up to its principles, but in the exposure of its inability to provide any absolute and disinterested standard for the conduct of international affairs.
>
> (Carr 1939: 88)

Carr's analysis of the failure of the League of Nations is much more than a scholarly critique of inter-war world politics. In fact it set the tempo for IR as a discipline. Carr started what came to be known as the first 'great debate' in IR (see Chapter 1). Carr's *The Twenty Years' Crisis* was unequivocal in its declaration:

> The exposure by realist criticism of the hollowness of the utopian edifice is the first task of the political thinker. It is only when the sham has been demolished that there can be any hope of raising a more solid structure in its place.
>
> (Carr 1939: 89)

Realism tells a story of the necessary limitations on global governance, a story that offers to help us understand the failures of the past and the possibilities for the present and future. Just as the story of Westphalia is the founding myth of the history of international politics so Carr's critique of the League provides the foundation for the debates in the theory of international relations. It is to these that we turn in Chapter 3.

TOPICS FOR DISCUSSION

1 Why is the states system taken to be the object of study of modern world politics?
2 Why is the modern states system taken to be anarchical?
3 What are the principal characteristics of a *sovereign* state?
4 How did the Westphalian system become the international system?
5 Does the anarchical character of the international system limit our options in terms of international political action?
6 In what sense is the balance of power the key to understanding modern IR?
7 Did the League of Nations represent a fundamental break with the Westphalian system of IR?

FURTHER READING

Most textbooks will have sections on the development of the modern states system. It is also useful to get used to reading the shorter essays that are published in academic journals. They are often more complex but represent the cutting edge of research and debate. The following list includes books that focus on specific themes relevant to this section and some of those articles that offer critical perspectives on these themes.

GENERAL

Watson, A. (1992) *The Evolution of International Society: A Comparative Historical Analysis*, London: Routledge.

ON WESTPHALIA

Osiander, A. (2001) 'Sovereignty, International Relations and the Westphalian Myth', *International Organization*, 55 (2): 251–287.

Gross. L. (1948) 'The Peace of Westphalia, 1648–1948', *American Journal of International Law* 42 (1): 20–41.

ON INTERNATIONAL LAW

Cassese, A. (2001) *International Law*, Oxford: Oxford University Press.

ON THE BALANCE OF POWER

Sheehan, M. (1996) *The Balance of Power: History and Theory*, London: Routledge.

ON DIPLOMACY

Berridge, G.R. (2002) *Diplomacy: Theory and Practice*, Basingstoke: Palgrave.

REALISM

The basics

The realist criticisms of the utopianism of the post-war liberal agenda were to have an enormous influence on the study of IR (see Chapter 1). In order to appreciate this we need to begin to think in a little more detail about what realism is and why it had such an impact on our subject. In order to achieve this goal this chapter will concentrate primarily on realist schools of thought examining their appeal and principal contributions to our understanding of modern and contemporary world politics. An engagement with realism necessarily entails an exploration of some of the principal opponents of the realist position. In Chapter 4 we will look at the one school of thought, developed in opposition to realism, which can be said to be mainstream or traditional in the same way as realism. Looking at the positions of realists and liberals will give us the opportunity to explore the applicability of realism to contemporary international politics. It will also preface our introduction to the rise of non-state actors in world politics, to globalization and to contemporary approaches to IR in later chapters. Your view of the world is coloured by the assumptions that you bring to it. It is thus essential that we lay out some of the most common assumptions so that you can critically engage with them.

REALISM: THE SCIENCE OF POWER POLITICS

One of the principal reasons that realism has been such an enduring approach in IR is because it sets itself up as a 'no-nonsense' practical science of international politics. Another reason is that its central tenets are clear and easy to grasp and seem to have immense explanatory power. By this we mean that the way that realists explain the forces that drive foreign policy seems to fit neatly with those aspects of world politics that we explored in Chapter 2. One of the most striking ways in which this is the case is the way that the realists argue that any objective analysis of international affairs must focus on power relations between states. This seems to allow them to 'cut through' utopian political rhetoric and to focus on the 'realities' of the situation. This appears to give realists a powerful starting point. For example, Carr's critique of inter-war liberalism shows that the concerns for peace and justice articulated by Wilson, Eden and Briand were articulations of the national interest of the victorious allies and that the enlightenment ideals of cosmopolitanism and humanitarianism, upon which their liberalism was based, were, when they were developed in the seventeenth and eighteenth centuries, themselves plans to perpetuate an international status quo favourable to the French monarchy (Carr 1939: 85–87; see also Chapter 2). In making these claims Carr shows that a realistic grasp of the situation requires, above all else, an analysis of power. Later Morgenthau (1948) was to argue that the concept of power 'provides the link between reason trying to understand international politics and the facts to be understood'.

> The concept of interest defined as power imposes intellectual discipline upon the observer, infuses rational order into the subject matter of politics and thus makes the theoretical understanding of politics possible. On the side of the actor, it provides for rational discipline in action and creates that astounding continuity in foreign policy which makes American, British or Russian appear as in intelligible, rational continuum, by and large consistent within itself, regardless of the different motives, preferences, and intellectual and moral qualities of successive statesmen.
>
> (Morgenthau 1948: 5)

The first key feature of realist international theory is, then, the focus on power.

This can be refined further by recognising that realists limit their enquiries to the study of state power. Realists emphasise the fact that states are the primary actors or the centres of power in world affairs. This means that the language of 'power politics' helps us explain state action. All else (the study of regional and international organizations, or of economics or law) is ultimately of secondary importance. This does not mean that it is not interesting or worthy of study. It simply means that any search for the essence of world affairs will eventually be reduced to power relations between nation-states. If, for example, you want to understand the character of international law, or of IGOs such as the UN, you will eventually have to understand them in terms of the power of states. This claim to be 'realistic', to 'cut to the chase', is why the realists gave themselves this title. Admittedly calling yourself a realist and branding your intellectual and political opponents 'utopians' tends to skew the rhetoric of any debate but as a stroke of academic *realpolitik* it worked magnificently. Sharing a concern to focus on the realities of power politics leads realists to share other core ideas such as attempts to understand statecraft (strategies for gaining power), the nature of the security dilemma facing actors in world politics (threats to power), the ways in which configurations of power change over time (the balance of power). What emerges is something like a manual for understanding and conducting international politics and this is another of the great appeals of the tradition.

A further attractive feature of realism is its claim to be engaged in a practical science of politics. As we shall see in an exploration of some of the key figures in the realist school the tradition aspires to scientific rigor, to the generation of objective laws (Morgenthau 1948: 4), to the theoretical elaboration of laws that are provable by observation and experiment (Waltz 1979: 5–7). When we are dealing with something as vital as national survival surely we want to premise our thought and action on 'the truth' about the world. We will return to the complex idea of what counts as truth and how we discover it later. Nevertheless the ambitions of the realist tradition to discover the timeless laws of world politics and to elaborate prescriptive theories based on those laws are an important feature of the dominance of the approach.

The common themes of realism, then, are the necessary anarchy of the state of nature, the self-interest of power hungry actors, the priority of power over morality or justice, the importance of the state as prime actor, and the claim that examining these themes leads to a realistic or scientific account of the world of IR. Despite this unity it is important to recognize that there are clear differences between various forms of realism and a myriad of complex subtleties that mark one important work from another.

THE INTELLECTUAL HISTORY OF REALISM

Realism claims a rich and venerable history. The core themes of realism, it is argued, are to be found repeatedly in some of the classical works in the history of political thought. In Machiavelli, as we saw in Chapter 2, we find clear expression of the ideas of power politics, necessity, reason of state and the primacy of politics over ethics. Machiavelli was writing at the birth of the modern state but the history of these key features of relations between organized political units is much older. The realists often draw attention to the work of Thucydides' whose *The Peloponnesian War* tells the history of the war between the Athenian Empire and Sparta and her allies that was fought between 431 and 404 BC. Key passages in this ancient work include the Melian Dialogue where the powerful Athenians threaten the Melians who despite their military inferiority trust in the Gods to support them in their struggle for 'what is right against what is wrong'. The Melians held out for some time but ultimately they were crushed, the grown men were killed, women and children sold as slaves and Melos inhabited by Athenian colonists. The moral of the story, made clear by the Athenian justification for their actions is 'that right, as the world goes, is only in question between equals in power, while the strong do what they can and the weak suffer what they must' (Thucydides, *The Peloponnesian War*, Book 5, 1972, Chapter 17). Power, then, trumps justice and morality.

The realists also claim one of the most striking political images of the modern world for their own. Thomas Hobbes was an English political theorist writing at the time of the English Civil War. His greatest work (*Leviathan*, written during the English civil war and published in 1651) is most famous for its account of how human beings act in the absence of government. This anarchical situation he calls the state of nature and he shows that in this state of nature humans are roughly equal in terms of power in that each person has an equal chance at getting what they desire at the expense of others. Concepts of right and wrong, justice and injustice, have no place in the state of nature being ideas that require the authority and power of a sovereign to develop and uphold. In this condition humans are compelled by their very nature, by fear and reason, by the security dilemma they face, to act selfishly. Indeed force and fraud are the two cardinal virtues of action. In one of the most famous quotations in the history of politics Hobbes summarizes the consequences of anarchy and equality writing:

> Hereby it is manifest that during the time men live without a common power to keep them all in awe, they are in that condition which is called war; and such a war as is of every man against every man. For war consisteth not in battle only, or the act of fighting, but in a tract of time, wherein the will to contend by battle is sufficiently known.
>
> (Hobbes, *Leviathan*, Chapter 13, 1996: 185–186)

For Hobbes the state of nature is necessarily a state of war and if we think of what happened in England during the Civil War period of the middle of the sixteenth century or in Kosovo in the twentieth century we can see the human disaster that seems inevitably to follow the absence of government. For Hobbes this terrible situation can be resolved only by submitting to the authority of an all powerful sovereign (the Leviathan of the title). But this option is not available (or even attractive) on an international scale. As a consequence anarchy, equality and war are taken to be the key features of world politics (which is routinely referred to as a state of nature), force and fraud the most sensible forms of action and morality nowhere to be seen. A realistic look at human and state interactions under conditions of anarchy requires that we recognise this, take it as given and proceed from this acknowledgment to our explanation of world politics. We must learn from history and from some of the greatest political analysts of history that a clear understanding of international affairs requires that we accept the realities and limitations of politics (Box 3.1).

BOX 3.1 REALISM IN THE HISTORY OF IDEAS

	Principal work	Realist ideas
Thucydides	*The History of the Peloponnesian War,* 431 BCE	Power versus justice Necessity
Machiavelli	*The Prince,* 1513	Necessity Reason of state Morality subservient to politics
Hobbes	*Leviathan,* 1651	Human nature The state of nature as a war of all against all Power Morality as a political concept

CLASSICAL REALISM: HUMAN NATURE AND THE STATE IN INTERNATIONAL RELATIONS

One of the most common ways of distinguishing between two of the major realist approaches is to draw a line between 'classical' or 'traditional' realism and 'neo' or 'structural' realism. In essence the classical realists argue that human nature causes states to act in certain ways and the structural realists argue that the system of international politics is the causal motor of world politics. In exploring classical and structural realism we will be looking at very different arguments in favour of adopting a realist approach to the study of IR.

MORGENTHAU'S CLASSICAL REALISM

Classical realism has, we suggested, a rich history. Morgenthau's (1948) *Politics among Nations* developed these key themes and applied them to world politics after the Second World War and it was to have an enormous impact on generations of practitioners and scholars. The best place to begin a basic outline of Morgenthau's realism is with an examination of his famous 'Six Principles of

Political Realism' (which appear in the second and later editions of this book).

MORGENTHAU'S SIX PRINCIPLES

1 Political realism believes that politics, like society in general, is governed by objective laws that have their roots in human nature.
2 The main signpost that helps political realism find its way through the landscape of international politics is the concept of interest defined in terms of power.
3 Realism assumes that its key concept of interest defined as power is an objective category which is universally valid.
4 Political realism is aware of the moral significance of political action. . . . while the individual has the moral right to sacrifice himself in defense of [such] a moral principle, the state has no right to let its moral disapprobation . . . get in the way of successful political action, itself inspired by the moral principle of national survival.
5 Political Realism refuses to identify the moral aspirations of a particular nation with the moral laws that govern the universe. . . . To know that nations are subject to the moral law is one thing, while to pretend to know with certainty what is good and evil in the relations among nations is quite another. . . . it is exactly the concept of interest defined in terms of power that saves us from moral excess and that political folly.
6 The political realist maintains the autonomy of the political sphere, as the economist, the lawyer, the moralist maintain theirs.

(Morgenthau 1985 [1948]: 4–14)

The key message that we can draw from the whole approach is that realism is necessarily a simplification of the world. It is intended to close off a manageable area of study and to focus on its core features rather than to be an exhaustive theory of world affairs. Politics is to be considered distinct from law, morality and economics and we are asked to focus on the basic concept of political interaction (power) as opposed to the basic concepts of law, morality or economics (point 6). There is also the idea that politics is somehow more realistic than the other disciplines which must cleave to the political.

HUMAN NATURE

Morgenthau's contribution to the realist tradition must be assessed in terms of three key ideas – human nature, power and interest – and one general theme, the balance of power. The idea that human nature is fixed and has a defining impact on the way we conduct world politics is an interesting one. If world politics is simply human nature 'writ large' we must work out what human nature is. The realist view is that human nature is inherently self-interested which gives us a tendency to conflict. The history of political thought is littered with competing yet compelling accounts of human nature. The Hobbesian account of human nature that features so heavily in the realist tradition is challenged in its entirety by those who see compassion, morality, sociability rather than fear and self-interest as key features of human nature. There are, of course, plenty of examples of humans behaving appallingly to one another. What you must consider is whether this is something that is necessarily a feature of human nature and therefore something that we must take in to account when thinking about how states will act in world affairs. This requires that you accept that we can discover what human nature is and that it is fixed. It also requires that you accept that it is human nature and not our social and political context that determines how we act.

INTEREST DEFINED IN TERMS OF POWER

The key argument for classical realists is that human nature is egoistical or selfish and therefore we should concentrate on how humans pursue their own interests. Focusing on how humans acquire the power to satisfy their interests thus gets right to the heart of the matter. Recall now Morgenthau's third principle. He goes on to argue that both the concept of interest and the concept of power are abstract ideas. There is no timeless or universal understanding of interest or what humans desire and no timeless and universal understanding of the means to attaining the objects of interest. Interest and the tools of power will differ over time and over history. Nevertheless we can be assured that humans will attempt to achieve their interests and will employ whatever power is at their disposal to do so. Because we can make this assumption we can define interest in terms of power. A state that is very powerful will have interests consistent with that power. The ability of a powerful state to stand above the compromises of world politics or to dictate its terms using its navy, genuine nuclear capability or merely its economic and political self-sufficiency is well evidenced by history. For this reason it is important, argued Morgenthau, to understand the elements of power which he lists as geography, natural resources, industrial capacity, military preparedness, population, national character and morale, and quality of diplomacy and government (Morgenthau 1985: 127–169). The pessimism that comes from the recognition that states will act on interests that are limited solely by their relative power is clear but should not be overstated. Morgenthau is clear that a realist grasp of the facts of international politics has had, and could continue to have, genuine benefits for the stability of international society. Indeed he sees the balance of power, based on an intellectual and moral consensus in the community of nations (Morgenthau 1985: 237, 240), as the mechanism that sustains such stability.

STRUCTURAL REALISM

The fundamental premise of Morgenthau's realism is, as we have seen, his account of human nature and this has clear policy implications for the foreign policy maker. The other dominant tradition in realist writing rejects this account arguing that focusing on the character and decision-making of actors in IR is to misunderstand the real causal factors in IR. The key criticism is not (just) that it is difficult to pin down human nature with any scientific rigor. The banner headline of this second realist tradition, a tradition most closely associated with Kenneth Waltz, is simply that it is the structure of the system and not the character of the units that determine the nature of world politics. In other words even if human nature was generous and giving we would still be compelled to act selfishly such is the nature of international politics.

AGENT OR STRUCTURE – LEVELS OF ANALYSIS

One way of thinking about IR is in terms of the idea that all social explanation can be reduced to the level of individual actors – we can look at the role of key individuals, the choices that they made, their intentions, their aims and from there we can create an account of world events. In doing this we are arguing that certain choices and decisions made by different people at different times are the things that we need to be looking at in explaining international relations. This kind of approach to international relations then would emphasise the *agency* of individual actors – the ability of individuals to make choices and determine their own outcomes.

For many scholars of IR this is not enough because people want to be able to understand not just one specific incident – but they want to identify trends and patterns in behaviour – they want to see whether there is something out there that actually conditions the way in which individuals behave. To do this, a number of social science researchers have identified the *structures* that inform the agency of the individual actors. Their argument is that *Actions are always conditioned upon (a response to/caused by) a certain context, and those actions can only be fully understood in relation to that context.*

This context is often referred to as a structure, because it *shapes* the behaviour of individuals (or in the case of neo-realism, states). So to take an example, the *structure of a house* – its basic framework, the girders and foundations that hold the house up – shapes the way in which that house ultimately looks. It's the same sort of thing when we talk about social structures – these are the frameworks in which our behaviour takes place – the difference between social structures and the structure of a house is that social structures are invisible.

You will discover through the course of your studies here that certain theories place great emphasis on these invisible structural elements. These kinds of theorists make the suggestion that social analysis needs to look beneath the visible, observable world to understand how particular structures are *made, sustained and operated.*

WALTZ AND THE CONSTRAINTS OF ANARCHY

When he wrote the hugely influential *Theory of International Politics* Waltz was concerned both to provide a rigorously scientific account of 'theory' and to remedy the defects of existing IR theories. The feature that all these previous theories share is that they are, in a variety of ways, 'reductionist'. Reductionist theories, in Waltz's use of the term, fail to take adequate account of the systemic or structural determinants of international politics. Typically this is because IR theorists focus on the character of the interacting units (states) rather than on how the structure of the system in which they interact controls or constrains their actions. In simple reductionist theories (such as Morgenthau's) the analysis might focus on the quality of a country's diplomatic service or its ideology (Waltz 1979: 58; see also Waltz 1959). The central reason that Waltz rejects such approaches becomes very clear as he writes,

> When and how internal forces find external expression, if they do, cannot be explained in terms of the interacting parties if the situation in which they act and interact constrains them from some actions, disposes them towards other, and affects the outcomes of their interactions.
>
> (Waltz 1979: 65)

If we focus on unit level analysis (state behaviour, decision-making processes and power) it quickly becomes clear that we cannot explain everything that happens in IR. In particular we risk ignoring system level causal factors. How, asks Waltz, can we account for persistent similarities of outcome where actors vary? The answer lies in the recognition that 'the enduring anarchic character of international politics accounts for the striking sameness in the quality of inter-national life through the millennia' (Waltz 1979: 66).

Waltz shows that political structures can be defined by looking at three core elements:

> [F]irst by the principle according to which they are organized or ordered, second by the differentiation of the units and the specification of their functions, and third by the distribution of capabilities across units.
>
> (Waltz 1979: 88)

Political structures can be organized in two ways. They can be centralized and hierarchical (like domestic political structures) or they can be decentralized and anarchical (which is clearly the case in international politics). The fact of anarchy necessarily implies that the units that populate the system (in this case states) must be treated as fundamentally similar. To say that states are the same is 'another way of saying that states are sovereign' (Waltz 1979: 95) and that states control or define the nature of the system in a way that international organizations, transnational movements and multinational corporations do not. It is a claim about the function of the units rather than a claim that states are equal or uniform: 'states are alike in the tasks that they face, though not in their abilities to perform them' (Waltz 1979: 96). Here then we are still focused on a rather abstract account of the structure of the international political system which is a very good thing when we are trying to say how units stand in relation to one another. However, the third core element of Waltz's approach does begin to distinguish between the units as he examines the ways in which the units are distinguished by their greater or lesser capacities for performing similar tasks (Waltz 1979: 97). Here Waltz looks at the distribution of capabilities or relative power. The reason that Waltz looks at variations in power (rather than differences in national character, ideology or form of government etc.) is because the distribution of capabilities is itself a system-wide concept. Waltz's method, in a nutshell, is quite simple.

> We abstract from any particular qualities of states and from all of their concrete connections. What emerges is a positional picture, a general description of the overall arrangement of a society written in terms of the placement of units rather than in terms of their qualities.
>
> (Waltz 1979: 99)

What we find when we look at the world of IR through this theoretical lens is that the system (and hence the way it informs the actions of states) varies to a significant degree only when the distribution of capabilities changes from a world in which there are a number of states with the power to achieve their goals in IR to one in which there are only two states capable of such action. Structural realism pays very close attention to the overall architecture of the system. In a multipolar world (where there are several great powers) the security competition is likely to be different from a bipolar world (where there are only two great powers). This insight was of particular importance as Waltz tried to assess the prospects for peace and stability in a Cold War world with two nuclear superpowers in competition and it continues to be vital as we attempt to make sense of the security competition in a post-Cold War era.

DEFENSIVE AND OFFENSIVE REALISM

Waltz (1979) argued that states are forced to compete with each other for power because they desire security. His theory has been labelled 'defensive realism' because he argues that states seek power only in order to achieve security and will stop trying to achieve relative advantage over others because it will motivate others to join together in alliances against them. Defensive realism is contrasted with the more recent structural-realism of Mearsheimer (2001), whose 'offensive realist theory' argues that the structure of the international system provides 'powerful incentives for states to look for opportunities to gain power at the expense of rivals'. In contrast to Waltz's view that a state's goal is survival Mearsheimer argues that 'a state's ultimate goal is to be a hegemon in the system' (Mearsheimer 2001: 21). That structural-realism can produce such different theories may seem odd. But they are still both theories about how an anarchical system compels states to seek power for their survival. Waltz and Mearsheimer are suggesting that different strategies work best. A theory is just that, a theory, and the project of realists in IR is to test that theory against the world by amassing evidence that supports or falsifies the theoretical claims. The more evidence we amass the more confidently we can make our assertions about how states act in given circumstances. In particular we want to know how stable a system is and when a security competition might erupt into war. Both Waltz and Mearsheimer claim that in a multipolar world, regardless of who or how many have the power to control the system, states are encouraged to act in one clearly identifiable manner and that in a bipolar world states act in a different manner. In any case, argues Waltz, in a gentle rebuke to those who followed him:

> Whether the best way to provide for one's security is by adopting offensive or defensive strategies varies as situations change. A state having too much power may scare other states into uniting against it and thus become less secure. A state having too little power may tempt other states to take advantage of it. Realism is best left without an adjective to adorn it.
>
> (Waltz 2004: 6)

REALISM AND THE BALANCE OF POWER

The shift from a multipolar world to a bipolar world immediately after the Second World War is one of the key features of the period when Waltz and Morgenthau were writing and it forms the backdrop for contemporary IR theorists who seek to understand the changing patterns of power in a post-Cold War world. The idea was that we could have a scientific theory that could predict the ways in which the two nuclear superpowers would act. Would the Cold War turn hot? Would the new found stability in Western Europe last? It was these central questions that realism promised to answer.

For realists the constant rivalry of states whose foreign policy is determined by their national interest is a permanent feature of the international system and an equally constant reordering of the balance of power is the only form of stability available in a system where sovereign independence is as valued (if not more so) as stability itself. Morgenthau, with his historical approach, argues that 'the balance of power and policies aiming at its preservation are not only inevitable but are an essential stabilizing factor in a society of sovereign nations' (Morgenthau 1985: 187). Waltz, from his theoretical perspective, also argues that the balance of power system of international politics is an inevitable consequence of its anarchical structure. Power balancing, he argues, is the tendency to form alliances with the weaker rather than the stronger in order to ensure first that no overall dominant power emerges and thereby to maximize security. The lesson we learn from history is that 'balancing, not bandwagoning, is the behaviour induced by the system. The first concern of states is not to maximize power but to maintain their positions in the system' (Waltz 1979: 126). Despite these shared views the difference between a unit level account and a system level explanation becomes clear in their analyses of balance of power in a bipolar system. Morgenthau believes that the balance of power and hence the stability of world order breaks down in a bipolar system. Waltz was concerned to show that when looked at from a systems perspective there is good cause to think that a more stable balance will be the result (Figure 3.1).

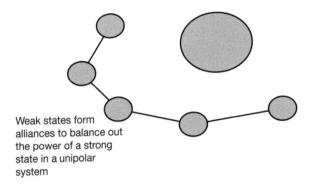

Weak states form
alliances to balance out
the power of a strong
state in a unipolar
system

Figure 3.1 Power balancing

MORGENTHAU AND THE BALANCE OF POWER

Despite 300 years of experience the balance of power is in danger of failing us in the twentieth century, argued Morgenthau. There are many reasons for the failure of the balance of power system in the contemporary era but these can be broken up in to two main categories; *structural* changes in the international system and *political* changes in the way nations seek to regulate their interactions. The structural changes coincide with the decline of Europe as the powerhouse of world politics. Morgenthau charted the gradual reduction in the number of nations who are able to play a meaningful role in the balance of power system of international politics from the hundreds of sovereign states in existence at the end of the Thirty Years War, to the eight great powers in existence at the outbreak of the First World War, to the bipolar system that emerged after the Second World War. The problem is that 'the flexibility of the balance of power and, with it, its restraining influence on the power aspirations of the main protagonists on the international scene have disappeared' (Morgenthau 1985: 363). In other words the key to understanding the instability of the bipolar world lies in understanding the way that structural changes alter the political manoeuvrings of the units. The superpowers (the USSR and the USA) did not need to pay attention to the manoeuvrings of their allies, there was no longer a 'balancer', a power that could tip things either way – a role that Great Britain had held for a considerable time. As a consequence the superpowers were locked in a 'balance of terror' based on the threat of mutually assured destruction (MAD) rather than a balance of power based on a moral consensus. At the same time the end of the colonial era brought further changes and yet more inflexibility. Without the 'empty political spaces' of the colonial frontiers conflicts once again centred on the nations of Europe and their populations and conflicting powers were unable to resort to territorial compensation (dividing up colonial territories) as a method of conflict resolution. These structural factors along with the industrialization of both political society and warfare led to the era of total war and, Morgenthau contended,

> Total war waged by total populations for total stakes under the conditions of the contemporary balance of power may end in world domination or world destruction or both.

> (Morgenthau 1985: 412)

The political developments that threatened the stability of world politics are summed up in Morgenthau's claim that contemporary politicians have failed to recognize that 'international peace cannot be preserved though the limitation of national sovereignty' (Morgenthau 1985: 563). The business of diplomacy, Morgenthau readily admits, is not as 'spectacular, fascinating, or inspiring' as the grand designs of collective security, international government or even international socialism that have been proposed as solutions to the tensions of contemporary world politics. However, the simple fact is that all these proposals rely on the ideal of an integrated international society which does not exist and, if we are to take Morgenthau's account of human nature seriously, is unlikely to ever come in to existence. Morgenthau's final word lays out nine rules of diplomacy. These rules recognize that the threats to peace that stem from structural changes to the international arena are irreversible and that the only independent variable is the tendency to nationalistic universalism – Morgenthau's term for the drive to impose one vision of political life, whether communist or liberal, upon the whole world. Giving up on this kind of political ambition is the only way to re-engage in the 'community building processes' of diplomacy.

WALTZ AND THE BALANCE OF POWER

Morgenthau thought that the new balance of power lacked those features of a classical balance of power that lent it stability. Waltz on the other hand argues that the bipolar world was likely to be more stable. Waltz agreed with Morgenthau on the nature of the structural changes leading to bipolarity but because he wanted us to focus on the systemic pressures that guided state action rather than political changes to unit level decision-making he came to a very different conclusion. For Waltz, the dynamics of a two power system meant that the two powers are able to deal with each other more effectively. This is characteristic, he argued, of a small number system. The fewer the number of players (in a market system or in IR) the easier it is to reach, police and maintain agreements and the greater the incentive to maintain the system (Waltz 1979: 135–136). Because of this we have seen that ideological concerns give way to a conservative foreign policy, as the bid to universalize liberalism or communism was given up in favour of containment and compromise. There is also a curious benefit to be had from military stalemate brought on by the threat of mutually assured destruction. A multipolar system is a constant scene of adjustment and readjustment of power relations. The history of warfare between the great powers of Europe is surely to be contrasted with the history of compromise, stand-off and cooperation between the two superpowers. There are clear advantages to 'having two great powers, and only two, in the system' (Waltz 1979: 161). Famously Waltz argued that the bipolar system would long remain the world's most exclusive club. His reasoning was that the resources the superpowers control, the simplicity of relations between two rather than three or more parties and the strong pressures that are generated by this structure to respond to perceived threats to the balance of power breeds a dynamic stability. At the same time the barriers to other states attaining the levels of power of the USSR and the USA were so great that the prospect of a return to multipolarity were minimal. Essentially the Cold War was to set in.

BEYOND THE COLD WAR

The Cold War did not set in (at least when you compare the 40 year period of bipolarity with the 300 years of multipolarity following Westphalia). Nor did it end in nuclear Armageddon. The failure of realism to predict the end of the Cold War was greeted by many as a sure sign that the pessimism of classical realism and the systemic claims of neo-realism were wrong. Nevertheless Waltz, writing in 2004, defiantly claimed:

> The collapse of the Soviet Union was caused not by the triumph of liberal forces operating internationally but by the failure of the Soviet Communist System. The Cold War ended exactly as realists had predicted. The Cold War rooted in the bipolar system and would end only when that system collapsed.
>
> After the Cold War, does realism still reign? As the title of an essay by Robert Gilpin has it, 'Nobody Loves a Realist.' Yet time and again, from antiquity to the present, realism has emerged from the competition of explanations as the most useful comprehensive one for explaining outcomes produced by units existing in a condition of anarchy. As long as that condition endures, realist theory remains the most useful instrument for explaining international political events.
>
> (Waltz 2004: 6)

Mearsheimer (2001), writing with the benefit of hindsight, endorsed Waltz's view of the stability of great power politics in a bipolar world (Mearsheimer 2001: 356). He goes on to apply the logic of structural realism to an analysis of structure and peace in the 1990s to 'tomorrow's Europe'. Pouring scorn on the optimists who thought the end of the Cold War heralded a new and different world, Mearsheimer charts the role of American military power in containing a future great power war in Europe. He points to the prospect of Germany making a new bid for European hegemony, the rise of China as a great power in the East and ends with an injunction to the USA not to turn its back on 'the realist principles that have served it well since its founding' (Mearsheimer 2001: 402). In similar vein Desch (2003) shows that realism continues to have much to offer in respect of international crises. Whether the issue is ethnic cleansing in the Balkans, nuclear standoff over Kashmir, or the usefulness of economic sanctions as a tool of foreign policy realism remains a powerful explanatory force in contemporary IR (Desch 2003).

SOME BASIC CRITICISMS OF REALISM

Morgenthau and Waltz provide the foundations for the two principal traditions in contemporary realist IR theory. Much work has been done in both traditions, work that develops, updates, and sometimes directly challenges the substantive theories of these two authors. As you proceed from *The Basics* to a more complete investigation of realism in IR theory you will be able to identify those scholars who rely on a classical realist or a structural realist approach. Here, however, we need to focus our attention on some of the key ideas in realism theory that are often the subject of criticism.

First, there is a general issue with the use of terms such as power or national interest to describe the actions or motivations of states. Both forms of realism seek theoretical simplicity (or parsimony) in order to help us cut through the complex detail of world politics and reach a series of explanations. Yet there is sense in which if everything through history can be described in these terms it explains nothing. In elaborating on his third general principle of realism Morgenthau shows that.

> The idea of interest is indeed the essence of politics and is unaffected by the circumstances of time and place ... Yet the kind of interest determining political action in a particular period of history depends on the political and cultural context in which foreign policy is formulated. The same observations apply to the concept of power ... Power covers the domination of man by man. Both when it is disciplined by moral ends and controlled by constitutional safeguards ... and when it is that untamed and barbaric force which finds its laws in nothing but its own strength.
>
> (Morgenthau 1985: 10–11)

Similarly in suggesting that the operation of a multipolar balance of power system was the same from ancient Greece to 1945 Waltz risks explaining very little about the politics of that long period of time. Of course all theories intend to simplify the world. The question is whether realism goes too far and leads to oversimplification.

A second issue relates specifically to classical realism and to its very popular claim that human nature causes conflict. It is clear from history that human beings are capable of incredible acts of barbarity and selfishness. However, it has yet to be established (and philosophers have been trying for thousands of years) that this is caused by our unchanging and unchangeable nature. If we are not driven by nature to conflict rather than cooperation, to cruelty rather than compassion, then it is possible for us to make a choice about how we act. To be sure it is a difficult choice and one that might expose us politically. But if it is a genuine choice then it makes the world of difference to how we understand IR.

A third issue relates specifically to structural realism and in particular to the mechanistic pressures that, Waltz (2004) argues, can be seen to guide the international political system. Waltz was keenly aware that the charge of structural determinism could be levelled at his theory nevertheless there is a clear sense in which he wants us to think that, regardless of the wishes of states, the mechanics of the system will ensure that we arrive at a balance of power. Despite Waltz's claims that he was deliberately overemphasizing structural causes in IR (precisely because others had obscured it) IR theory has been left with a polarized set of debates that oppose unit level analyses with system level analyses. Structural realists argue that structures are the prime objects for study and thus that we can understand the whole of history until the Cold War as a multipolar balance of power (despite radical changes in the distribution of capabilities among the units that are the key players). Everything else that happened in this period is said to relate to subsystem changes at the unit level and so robbed of real significance. Not only that but also the underlying message is that balance of power is inevitable, no matter what we do or aspire to.

A fourth issue is the state-centric nature of realist theory. The fact of the existence of states and the need to ensure their survival is built into the heart of realist theory. Humanity has divided itself up in to communities for security and economic reasons for millennia and this is not in dispute. However, the sovereign nation-state is a feature of modernity and one that arose to answer a specific historical set of problems. Questions about the continued utility and moral right of sovereign nation-states seem to be a clear feature of the contemporary world. We face issues of secession (the break up of states such as the former Soviet Union, the former Yugoslavia, and postcolonial states), questions concerning the rights of minority cultures and indigenous peoples, the political need to respond to abuses of human rights, to refugee crises and global poverty. Has the sovereign state outlived its usefulness and should we aspire to a greater political emphasis on regional and international governance? These questions cannot even be asked from a realist perspective.

A fifth issue relates to the subordination of moral claims to political claims in realist theory. As a claim about the need to simplify IR theory or to produce a science of IR the claim that we can discount morality is problematic. It is not so much the claim that political leaders have acted for the good of the state rather than for the moral good (whatever that might be) or that the progress of world politics is about relative power rather than justice that is the problem. It is the fact that a 'realistic' or serious grasp of international affairs should not concern itself with forming a moral judgement on these facts. A realist grasp of power politics might explain why we have not made real progress toward a world order capable of delivering on the human rights laid down in the Universal Declaration of 1948 but it cannot tell us whether or not we ought to move towards this goal. In fact it simply has not got the theoretical vocabulary to engage with the question and it is a question being pursued at the national, regional and international level.

A sixth criticism, and one that informs the neo-liberal institutionalism that we shall explore in Chapter 4, is that realism focuses on only one aspect of world politics to the detriment of others. Realists take the substance of IR to be great power politics, the 'high politics' of state competition, war and aggression. It is true that this is a key part of international relations but it is not the only aspect we need to look at. The realist perspective encourages the fallacy that to study IR is to study security. From this perspective we find that the hallmarks of international life are indeed competition and war. If, however, we broaden the scope of our studies to include economic relations, international development or international law our discoveries are rather different.

A final and more general point encompasses these criticisms and takes them to a more abstract critical level. In the contemporary academic literature critical theorists take the deep theoretical structure of realism and show how realism rests on a set of indefensible foundations that privilege certain contestable ideas in a way that protects them from critical scrutiny. Most theories have foundations. This is a technical term that refers to the basic assumptions about the nature of the world and how we come to know it (philosophers use the words ontology and epistemology here). The claim that lead to a theoretical revolution toward critical theory, constructivism and postmodernism was that it was not the nature of the world or international politics that lead us to believe that IR was the realism of repetition, selfishness, anarchy and conflict among states but that it was the way that realists put certain 'facts' about IR beyond critical scrutiny. We will explore this claim in much more detail in Chapter 5.

Are these good reasons not to adopt a realist approach to IR? To ignore realism is to ignore some important insights in to the conduct of world affairs. The problem is that some theories (and theorists) get carried away and make greater claims than those they are entitled to. In the polarized IR world of realists vs. idealists there is a tendency to treat realist theory as a complete world view rather than as an insightful simplification or model. Realism can tell us a lot about power politics but it is (or should be) silent in many other areas of IR. The claim that IR is the study of power relations between states, and only the study of power relations between states, excludes far too much that is of interest to the student of world affairs. Nevertheless a student of IR who ignored these relationships would clearly miss something vital.

TOPICS FOR DISCUSSION

1 What are the core principles of realism?
2 Describe the key differences between classical and structural realism.

3 Why do Morgenthau and Waltz differ on the stability of the balance of power in a bipolar world?
4 Which of the main criticisms of realism do you find compelling and why?

FURTHER READING

Most textbooks include a section on realism. Here we suggest you concentrate on reading the primary texts.

REALISM IN THE HISTORY OF POLITICAL THOUGHT

Thucydides (1972) *History of the Peloponnesian War*, (trans. R. Warner, Harmondsworth: Penguin.

Machiavelli, N. (1988) *The Prince*, ed. Q. Skinner and R. Price, Cambridge: Cambridge University Press.

Hobbes, T. (1996) *Leviathan*, ed. R. Tuck, Cambridge: Cambridge University Press.

A specialist textbook, such as Boucher, D. (1998) *Political Theories of International Relations*, Oxford, Oxford University Press, will help you in to this complex and rich literature.

CONTEMPORARY REALISM

Carr, E.H. (1939) *The Twenty Years' Crisis 1919–1939: An Introduction to the Study of International Relations*, London: Macmillan.

Waltz, K. (1979) *Theory of International Politics*, New York: McGraw-Hill.

Morgenthau, H.J. (1948) *Politics among Nations: The Pursuit of Power and Peace*, Chicago, IL: University of Chicago Press.

Mearsheimer, J. (2001) *The Tragedy of Great Power Politics*, New York: W.W. Norton.

4

LIBERALISM

The basics

Realism has had a tremendous impact on the study of international relations but it does have political and theoretical critics. It is, they argue, politically pessimistic, morally problematic, and methodologically reductivist. As long as there have been realists there have been criticisms of and alternatives to that tradition. A lot of the work we explore in the remaining chapters of this book stems from a reaction against realism's view of the limits and possibilities for international politics. In Chapters 5–7 we look at analyses of IR that emphasize interdependence and globalization and at those critical theories who refuse to take the world as they find it but attempt to think about how to transform it. As we have seen, the dominance of realism came at the expense of utopianism. Utopianism and idealism are terms used pejoratively to describe liberal approaches to IR. Despite being dismissed as utopian, liberalism is the historical alternative to realism and it is still thought to offer important insights in to the practices of international politics.

Like realism, liberalism is a very broad tradition comprising many distinct and often antithetical points of view. In IR textbooks liberalism is principally associated with the internationalism of inter-war liberals such as Wilson and, more recently, with the work of neo-liberal institutionalists such as Keohane and Nye (see Chapter

1). Liberalism is therefore described in broad terms as relying on claims about the impact of interdependence, the benefits of free trade, collective security and the existence of a real harmony of interests between states. In political theory or political philosophy liberalism is explored in significantly different terms. There liberalism is presented as a set of normative or moral claims about the importance of individual freedoms and rights. In recent work on global poverty and economic justice, humanitarian intervention, international law and human rights the normative element of liberalism is re-emerging as an essential part of liberal argument (see Chapter 8). A grasp of the basics of liberalism therefore requires both an understanding of the history of liberal institutionalism and an understanding of liberal ethics.

THE INTELLECTUAL HISTORY OF LIBERALISM

Because normative liberalism was sidelined for so long in IR, students are often not fully introduced to the intellectual history of liberalism. The study of ethics and morality is often ignored or thought of as properly the subject of a different class such as political theory which is rarely mandatory for students of IR. This is partly because realism rejected morality as irrelevant to the study of the proper subject of IR – power. However, the claim that IR is solely, or even primarily, the study of power is itself a contentious argument. Liberalism, in very broad terms, is a series of arguments about why we should study other aspects of world politics such as international law, human rights, economic cooperation or justice. Liberalism describes the very rich and diverse traditions of thought that ascribe real value to internationalism in political and international thought. For the canonical thinkers in this tradition morality has a key place in our political thinking as ultimately it is individuals, rather than states, that are important in international relations (as in all life). Theories that fall in to this broad tradition have very different reasons for their internationalism and see very different consequences flowing from their positions. Some liberals argue for the progressive development of international law, others for a reordering of the institutions of world politics on democratic or cosmopolitan lines, some urge a greater respect for human rights and global economic justice, others for a free market. To dismiss all liberal arguments as utopian is to dismiss a complex range of arguments that appear throughout the history of ideas in political and international thought.

LOCKE AND THE MORAL LAW IN THE STATE OF NATURE

Classic arguments that form the bedrock for many positions within this tradition can be very different. Indeed when searching for the *locus classicus* many introductory accounts of liberalism include the natural law theory of John Locke, the political theory of Immanuel Kant and the utilitarianism of Jeremy Bentham. Locke argued that the law of nature (the moral law) exists before politics as it is given by God (Locke II §6). The very fact that God makes us all equal means that we can work out the basic principles of politics such as natural rights to be free from any authority that we have not consented to or to own property. This law is absolute and trumps political necessity. Locke's is a seventeenth century expression of a very common idea. There is a moral law that precedes and trumps politics. In Locke's words the state of nature has a law of nature to govern it. Locke's description of the state of nature is fascinating. It is still anarchical but the injunction not to kill another human being still holds. Why wouldn't it? This is how we often think of moral rules. They still apply even when there is no one to enforce them. Locke therefore sees the anarchy of a state of nature as beset by what he calls in a rather understated manner 'inconveniences'. These inconveniences (such as the lack of an authoritative interpretation of the law of nature or the lack of a force to execute it) can be overcome politically *but only under conditions imposed by the moral law*. Locke's liberalism has been used to defend human rights and the global redistribution of wealth from the very rich to the very poor on the ground the rich had no right to simply take the wealth.

BENTHAM ON INTERNATIONAL LAW

Jeremy Bentham's approach was very different. Bentham was a leading figure in the philosophical school known as utilitarianism. Utilitarians argue that we should base our political judgements on something that we can measure. We could categorize things according to whether they tended 'to produce benefit, advantage, pleasure, good, or happiness ... or ... to prevent the happening of mischief, pain, evil, or unhappiness' (Bentham 1789: Introduction) and we should thus organize our political lives so as to achieve 'the greatest happiness of the greatest number' or by maximizing utility. For Bentham the concept of utility gives content to categories such as good and bad or right and wrong. Bentham argued that while nations were vitally important (it is within the state that the utility of individuals should be promoted) the project of constructing international law should sacrifice the ideal of national self-interest to the universal ideal of 'the greatest happiness of all nations taken together' (Essay One: The Objects of International Law at http://www.la.utexas.edu/research/poltheory/bentham/pil/pil.e01.html; see also Janis 1984: 415). In the fourth essay of *Principles of International Law* entitled 'A Plan for Universal and Perpetual Peace', Bentham argues, among other things, for an international court with powers resembling the Permanent International Court of Justice that was established under the League of Nations and the International Court of Justice of the United Nations. The court, he argues, is an obvious solution to the ridiculous costs of turning to warfare to settle disputes and changes nothing about the international system or the sovereignty of nations. There is no suggestion that the court would become an all powerful sovereign authority in its own right but in merely making its judgement and circulating its opinion it would likely make a significant difference to the need to resort to force. Indeed, Bentham argues, if you contrast the utility of warfare as conflict resolution with judicial arbitration as conflict resolution the calculation is not a particularly difficult one to make (Essay Four: A Plan for Universal and Perpetual Peace, proposition XIII, http://www.la.utexas.edu/research/poltheory/bentham/pil/pil.e04.html).

KANT ON INTERNATIONAL FEDERATION

Of all the enlightenment theories it is Kant's that forms the touchstone for the largest range of contemporary liberal arguments. Kant argued that we have an absolute duty to treat human beings as autonomous moral agents. Moral imperatives are categorical rather than instrumental – we act morally because we *ought* to and not because it brings us benefits. We have a moral duty, Kant argued, to structure our political and social lives (and this includes international politics) in a way that provides the basic conditions that make this moral goal possible. His work argues for a critical moral theory and proposes a political solution to the anarchical condition of world affairs. It has been developed in recent years to provide an account of individual rights, an argument for the importance of democratic institutions to peace, and arguments in favour of global distributive (economic) justice.

Kant is the most famous of all cosmopolitan philosophers. The title cosmopolitan comes from the Greek words *cosmos* (world) and *polis* (city) and refers to the idea that there is or should be a universal community of humankind (either moral or political). The argument that was to have such a huge impact of liberalism in IR was that there must be a political and institutional solution to the problem of international anarchy. The heart of Kant's moral philosophy was that the presumption of individual freedom (autonomy) was essential to all practical reason and to all morality. Kant argues that we have a categorical imperative or an absolute obligation to respect the autonomy of others and that failure to do this is the source of conflict.

For Kant the primary causes of conflict are the inherent instability and injustice of a state of nature. Establishing peace is therefore about overcoming the state of nature. Here, of course, Kant has made the same diagnosis for the principal ailment of international relations as the realists. It is anarchy that causes war. Realists go on to argue that nothing can or should be done to mitigate this anarchy. Why does Kant believe that we can and must overcome anarchy where the realists do not? Partly it is because Kant, and other liberals, believe that reason will prevail. We can usefully contrast this with the Hobbesian-realist view that fear, not reason, will prevail. This is to contrast the optimism of liberalism with the pessimism of realism. For a long time it has looked as though world politics is trapped in a cycle of fear, distrust and repetitive war. But to point to this is to confuse cause and effect. Anarchy causes fear and distrust. A just legal and political regime can break that cycle exposing a genuine harmony of interests. Kant's programme for 'perpetual peace' was an outline of such a regime. At the domestic level we require republican political constitutions where individual citizens are accorded equal standing. Internationally we can end the state of nature by entering in to a confederation of republican states under the law of nations. Globally we could establish a cosmopolitan law of peoples under which individuals gain certain rights internationally. Eventually, argued Kant in 1795, the war-weary peoples of Europe would realize this and begin to build a confederation of republican states with a further cosmopolitan order that would end war between them. And, so one could argue, they did in the construction of the European Union with the most highly functioning human rights regime in existence. The other reason why Kant saw peace through politics was because the injunction to leave the state of nature was not merely instrumental. Rather it was a categorical, moral *ought*. Ending the state of nature is to establish the political conditions under which humans can live morally, respecting the freedom of all others thus eliminating the primary source of conflict.

The idea that individuals are morally important is an idea that we are all familiar with. After all it is central to the idea of human rights that forms the core of post Second World War international politics. If individual rights really are universal and absolute then nothing justifies actions and institutions that threaten those rights. Of course there are times or circumstances when we cannot live up to moral standards but morality is still a guide to action. We do not have any real problem saying that genocide or other gross violations of human rights are wrong no matter what the circumstances. But this entails that we have reasons for valuing human beings and believing that they ought to be free from the tyranny of political oppression or, in more recent neo-Kantian arguments, even the tyranny of poverty and disease (see Chapter 8). If we take this seriously than we find that we have a duty to build institutions that guarantee this freedom. This, in fact, is a clear moral and legal position in our current political practices. Why then should we accept that power rather than morality should be the guide to international politics?

LIBERALISM TODAY

There is much more to be gained from an engagement with the work of Locke, Bentham and Kant (Box 4.1). There is still more from a more sustained exploration of broadly liberal ideas in international

BOX 4.1 LIBERALISM IN THE HISTORY OF IDEAS

John Locke, 1632–1704	*Two Treatises on Government*, 1688	Natural law	Economic rights Human rights
Jeremy Bentham, 1748–1832	*Introduction to the Principles and Morals of Legislation*, 1789 *Principles of International Law*, 1789	Utilitarianism	International law
Immanuel Kant, 1724–1804	*Perpetual Peace*, 1795 *Groundwork of the Metaphysics of Morals*, 1785	Transcendental idealism Categorical imperative	Cosmopolitanism Federation of Republican States

relations (see Boucher 1998; Brown 2002; Keene 2005). However, a basic guide to liberalism can do no more than show how this, the classical heritage of liberalism, feeds in to current debates. We can divide contemporary liberalism into two camps. The first form of liberalism draws on structural claims that the liberal institutions impact on international relations in specific ways. Here we find the bulk of liberal IR theory including the famous 'democratic peace thesis' and the most prominent form of liberalism in IR, neo-liberal institutionalism. The second form of liberalism is normative or cosmopolitan liberalism and includes a growing literature on just war and humanitarian intervention and distributive justice.

THE DEMOCRATIC PEACE THESIS

Michael Doyle famously picks up on one of Kant's insights to argue in favour of what has become known as the democratic peace thesis. Writing in 1983 Doyle argued:

> Conventions of mutual respect have formed a cooperative foundation
> for relations between liberal democracies of a remarkably effective kind.
> *Even though liberal states have become involved in numerous wars with*
> *nonliberal states, constitutionally secure liberal states have yet to engage*
> *in war with one another.*
>
> (Doyle 1983a: 214, original emphasis)

Doyle's is an empirical claim that draws on two of Kant's core ideas.
The first is that republican constitutions limit the warlike ambitions
of states to the extent that liberal states only go to war for good
liberal reasons (Doyle 1983a: 230). The internally liberal character
of a state means that there is an in-built respect for individual rights
and freedoms. Furthermore the consent of the citizens is required
for war to be declared and given that it is the citizens who both fight
and foot the bill for war they are likely to be reluctant. Both of these
factors help explain why liberal states are less warlike than the
princedoms of modern Europe. Second, in a society of liberal states
there is no good reason for going to war with another liberal state.
Liberal states share certain moral and political principles in common
and if one state regards another as just or good then there is no
reason to behave aggressively towards them. The idea is that the
moral and political message of Kant's *Perpetual Peace* (1795) is more
than a rather nice theory. The constitutional structure of liberal state
makes them 'realistically different' (Doyle 1983a: 235).

This argument has spawned a large number of empirical studies
of the relations between democratic states. The assertion that the
pattern of relations between democratic states shows that they do
not go to war with one another has been described as 'as close to
anything we have to an empirical law in international relations' (Levy
1989: 270 cited in Chan 1997: 60). As more and more countries
become democratic this observation becomes ever more significant.
The democratic peace thesis has found its way into the rhetoric of
powerful policy-makers such as the US President Bill Clinton (Owen
1994: 87) and is recognized as a real challenge to realism (Mearsheimer
2001: 367). Put most simply we can see that if the democratic peace
hypothesis can be established as a fact then the realist claim that
international anarchy is the structural cause of conflict is false. Of
course it might simply be that democratic states have not gone to

war with each other *yet*. We also have to be wary of the urge to use this empirical information to impose democracy across the globe or to crusade for liberalism (Doyle 1983b: 324). Nevertheless this form of liberalism is central to contemporary IR.

NEO-LIBERAL INSTITUTIONALISM

However, the dominant form of liberalism in the field of IR makes structural claims that go even further than the democratic peace thesis. Neo-liberal institutionalism offers a political science of international interdependence, a description of the relations between state and non-state actors in the anarchical environment of world politics. The primary reason that this school of thought qualifies for the title liberal is because its members argue that international politics has more opportunities for sustained cooperation. In making their case neo-liberal institutionalists challenge some of the basic assumptions of realism. However, as we shall see, neo-liberal institutionalism also has a lot in common with neo-realism.

The core idea that drives neo-liberalism is complex interdependence. Complex interdependence is the term that describes,

> a world in which actors other than states participate directly in world politics, in which a clear hierarchy of issues does not exist and in which force is an ineffective instrument of policy.
>
> (Keohane and Nye 1977: 24)

Each of these claims is important. The first claim challenges the state-centric analysis of realism arguing that in reality there are 'multiple channels' of political interaction. This means that a proper science of IR must look at the role of international organizations such as multinational corporations, international governmental organizations and international non-governmental organizations, as well as established norms and networks when trying to determine outcomes in world affairs. Take, for example, power or the ability to influence outcomes. A neo-realist such as Waltz would ask you assess the relative power of states or the distribution of capabilities among them – the thought being that the interests of the most powerful will prevail. Neo-liberal institutionalists such as Keohane and Nye (1977), on the other hand, ask you to look at *organizationally dependent capabilities*, such as voting power, ability to form coalitions, and control of elite networks: that is, by capabilities that are affected by the norms, networks and institutions associated with international organization.

(Keohane and Nye 1977: 55, original emphasis)

Here 'international organization' is a competing account of the structure of world politics, an ideal type that can usefully be contrasted with the model proposed by Waltz. The second claim, concerning the absence of a hierarchy of issues is equally important. Neo-liberal institutionalism concerns itself with 'low politics' (economic and social issues) as well as so called 'high politics' (security issues). International relations that deal with economic and social issues are an enormous part of IR and political relations of this kind are hugely significant to states. A state that prioritized security to the exclusion of economic cooperation (that is a state that acted in a manner consistent with realist predictions) is not only very rare but would also miss out on a range of advantageous cooperative opportunities. The claim here is both that neo-realists theory is wrong about what motivates states to act (because they establish a hierarchy of issues that prioritizes 'high' over 'low' politics) and that the dominance of realism is inhibiting cooperation on social and economic issues (because states have become socialized into thinking in realist terms). The final claim follows from these key ideas. Given complex interdependence it is obvious that military force is not of decisive relevance to all aspects of international relations. The claim is that realism excludes these important features of world affairs and in doing so exaggerates unhelpfully the conflictual nature of IR. We will examine the role of non-state actors in Chapter 5.

What marks neo-liberal institutionalists out from neo-realists, therefore, is the claim that international interdependence, fostered by the existence of international institutions, means that there is significant room for cooperation in international affairs. This, of course, appears to be in stark contrast to the state-centric view of inevitable international conflict we saw in neo-realism. It is hard to look at the politics among the nations of the European Union and other regional organizations without acknowledging that non-state actors are important. The key question is 'to what degree do international institutions promote cooperation rather than conflict?' Can we say that a state that pursues absolute gains by cooperating with others is more rational? The big debate between neo-realists such as Mearsheimer and neo-liberal institutionalists such as Keohane really develops this point. Both claim empirical evidence to back up their claims. Despite this clear difference between neo-realist and neo-liberal institutionalist approaches this form of theory has more in common with neo-realism than it does with traditional liberalism (Keohane 1988; Jervis 1999). Neo-liberal institutionalists accept the several key ideas that provide the basis of neo-realism. They accept the view of IR as anarchical. They accept the claim that the sovereign state is the most important actor. They also accept the epistemological claims of neo-realism and therefore accept its methodology. What this means is that they accept an empiricist account of what is out there and how to go about finding out about it. This means that what counts as proper scholarship in IR has to conform to the scientific model of observation and experiment. As was the case with neo-realism this has the immediate effect of relegating moral questions from the scope of our inquiry. The aim is to describe the world with scientific accuracy – to generate testable theories that we can compare with the world. Given this how is it possible that the neo-liberal institutionalists see such a different world to neo-realists? As Jervis (1999) notes:

> Some of this difference reflects the issues that the schools of thought analyze. Neo-liberal institutionalists concentrate on issues of international political economy (IPE) and the environment; realists are more prone to study international security and the causes, conduct, and consequences of wars. Thus although it would be correct to say that one sees more conflict in the world analyzed by realist scholars than in the world analyzed by neo-liberals, this is at least in part because they study different worlds.
>
> (Jervis 1999: 45)

One conclusion that we might draw from this line of thought is that you cannot adopt an exclusively liberal or an exclusively realist approach to IR all the time. There are times when you need the insights that both offer. The suggestion that the neo-liberal institutionalists and neo-realists share an approach to IR but look at different aspects of world politics has further implications. It has become routine to think of the 'third great debate' between neo-realists and neo-liberals not as an inter-paradigm debate but as an intra-paradigm debate. The two schools of thought share a rationalist, scientific method that came to dominate IR as discipline. However, just as the neo-liberals argued that the realists offered an incomplete picture of what we should study in IR so another group of scholars argue that neo-neo synthesis artificially excludes some important issues from the study of IR and makes assumptions that skew our understanding of the limits and possibilities of international politics. The realists made certain assumptions (the state as only significant actor, the priority of high over low politics) that appeared to blind them to the importance of international organization in constraining or modifying state behaviour. Similarly, argue a range of critical thinkers, the assumption that IR must be studied scientifically allied to a rationalist and positivist account of what can count as objective scientific fact excludes a range of insights into what is important in IR. In Chapter 6 we explore the contributions of critical theory, postmodernism and feminism to the study of IR and show how different approaches to your subject offer different and important insights in to world affairs; insights ignored by the positivist neo-neo synthesis.

COSMOPOLITANISM

Cosmopolitan arguments have at their core a normative commitment to universalism and individualism. Cosmopolitans are not necessarily liberals, indeed there is a significant strand of cosmopolitanism running through Marxism and socialism. Nevertheless liberal cosmopolitanism is increasingly coming to dominate debates abut globalization, human rights, international law and global justice. The main form that liberal cosmopolitanism takes is neo-Kantianism. Neo-Kantians have taken core features of Kant's argument and gone on to explore the nature of cosmopolitan justice. In Kant's *Perpetual Peace* cosmopolitan justice was limited to the provision conditions of universal hospitality. In neo-Kantian theory this is developed to explore vitally important questions of global justice. Here scholars such as John Rawls, Thomas Pogge, Charles Beitz and Onora O'Neill ask what a moral obligation to treat all other human beings as free or as ends in themselves, rather than as a means to our ends (which is one of the ways Kant describes his vision of the moral law) obliges us to do about issues such as world poverty and famine or the rights of stateless persons such as refugees, and the nature and scope of universal human rights. The questions explored here are essential to world politics. Cosmopolitans construct and defend moral arguments that focus on the rights of individuals (and on the duty of individuals and communities to respect those rights). For example, Thomas Pogge, drawing on Kant, shows that we have a series of clear commitments to respect the dignity and worth of individuals. This much is relatively uncontroversial being embedded in the universal declaration of human rights. In article 28 of that same document we agreed that 'Everyone is entitled to a social and international order in which the rights and freedoms set forth in this Declaration can be fully realized.' Yet the international order which gives the final say on matters concerning refugee movement, environmental policy and economic justice to self-interested sovereign states conspicuously fails in this regard. Pogge's cosmopolitanism is representative of the tradition in that it offers a real critique of the prevailing international order. Pogge specifically demands a dispersal of sovereign authority to subnational, national, regional and international levels to enable us to more effectively meet our moral obligations to the world's poor (Pogge 2002).

Similarly utilitarianism has a clear voice in the debates surrounding global economic justice and globalization. Peter Singer's seminal 'Famine, Affluence and Morality' (Singer 1972), *Practical Ethics* (Singer 1979) and his more recent *One World: The Ethics of Globalization* (Singer 2002) offer powerful interventions in these key debates. His 1972 article starts from what appears to be an unproblematic analogy intended to throw light on the way the rich respond to famine. However, as Singer goes on to show, we get from this basic starting point to a utilitarianism with strong cosmopolitan implications:

> if I am walking past a shallow pond and see a child drowning in it, I ought to wade in and pull the child out. This will mean getting my

clothes muddy, but this is insignificant, while the death of the child
would presumably be a very bad thing.

The uncontroversial appearance of the principle just stated is
deceptive. If it were acted upon, even in its qualified form, our lives,
our society, and our world would be fundamentally changed.

(Singer 1972: 230–231)

Singer's point here is that it is fairly clear that when we can do good
at little or no cost to ourselves we ought to do so. In the context of
his article Singer shows that giving money to the starving Bengalis
is not a charitable act. Rather, like saving a drowning child at the
cost of muddy trousers, it is a duty. Similarly Singer shows elsewhere,
it seems obvious that 'as more and more issues demand global
solution, the extent to which any state can independently determine
its future diminishes' (Singer 2002:198).

Cosmopolitan liberalism is a clear challenge to realism. It rejects
the realist assumption that the survival of the inter-state system is
the essence of IR and it rejects the realist claim that power is the
only proper object of study for IR. The extent of the challenge posed
by cosmopolitanism to realist orthodoxy in IR has meant that, for
many years, IR failed to take any notice of the tradition. It simply
did not fit the social science model and as such was thought to be
incapable of the sort of cold, hard proof than any useful theory of
IR required. To a degree this has changed since the early 1990s.
Normative theory generally has enjoyed resurgence and cosmopolitanism has a significant voice within that debate. Nevertheless it is
still the case that realism and cosmopolitanism have no common
ground on which they could combine their efforts.

A MIDDLE WAY BETWEEN REALISM AND LIBERALISM?

One of the biggest problems with the debate between realists and
liberals is the tendency for there either to be a strict polarization of
positions or for the neo-realists and neo-liberals to work within
a shared intellectual paradigm. The reason this is a problem is
because it seems fairly obvious that a full understanding of world
politics requires insights from realism and liberalism. The polarization
of IR into realist and liberal camps is a product of at least two

interrelated factors. First, in any attempt to construct a theory that has significant explanatory power there is a tendency to exaggerate or over-emphasize the core idea that supports your favoured theory. It is certainly the case that the realists and the liberals that we have examined all recognize that the opposite theory has merits. Nevertheless in order to develop a testable hypothesis or highlight the key moral arguments these concessions are lost in a bid to be clear and concise or the desire to win a debate. Second, if the development of IR is presented as a series of inter-paradigm debates (see Chapter 1) the polarization of positions becomes deeply embedded in the intellectual structure of the discipline. There is a lot to be gained from an initial engagement with the debates between realism and liberalism. However, you need to be critical in your view of both the individual realist or liberal arguments and the idea that they must be thought of as two utterly distinct world views. This last idea is particularly important to contemporary critical approaches to IR and in Chapter 6 we will look at attempts to break out of the rationalist neo-neo synthesis and construct post-positivist theories of IR. Here we will introduce you to one tradition of international thought that has attempted to forge a middle way between the insights of realism and of liberalism.

The 'international society' approach to IR theory, often referred to as the 'English school' (Jones 1981) or the Grotian School (Wight 1991), exists outside the mainstream social science debates that dominate US international studies. Its own rich history is characterized by its attempts to avoid the polarization seen in the debates between realists and liberals and by its commitment to the study of what Hedley Bull, one of the school's most important contributors, called 'the anarchical society' (Bull 1995: 74–94). As this term suggests the English school approach recognizes that anarchy is a structural feature of international relations but also recognizes that sovereign states form a society that uses conceptions of order *and* justice in its rhetoric and its calculations. The approach thus looks at balance of power *and* international law, great power politics *and* the spread of cosmopolitan values. The great strength of the approach is its refusal to engage with the positivist methodological turn in IR. Rather than adopt a positivist social science approach to the study of world affairs it offers a 'methodologically pluralist' approach to IR drawing on the study of history, philosophy and law (Buzan 2001: 472). This open approach to IR is also, some argue, its greatest weakness as it does not set up a straightforward research model which can be tested against the world in a scientific manner (Finnemore 2001).

The international society theorists do not reject the insights of Hobbes or Kant. Rather they work with them, seeking ways to link their insights (rejecting claims to have exclusive insight into the 'real world' of IR) and incorporating the work of classical international lawyers such as Hugo Grotius and Emmerich Vattel. As with the other approaches to IR there is diversity within the tradition. Bull traced this diversity back to these intellectual forebears of the English school. Grotius is associated with the 'solidarist' wing of the school which has a significant optimism about the solidarity of states as the authors of international law. Contemporary writers on this side of the approach include Nicholas Wheeler whose *Saving Strangers* argues for an emerging norm of humanitarian intervention in contemporary international society (Bull 1969; Wheeler 2000). Grotian solidarism is distinct from Kant's cosmopolitanism. Indeed Kant referred to Grotius, along with other international jurists, as a 'miserable comforter' in his *Perpetual Peace* because of the way they accommodate the use of war under certain conditions. Vattel (another of the miserable comforters) is associated with the more conservative 'pluralist' side of the approach. The pluralists in the English school argue that while states can agree on certain aspects of international society the very character of international law limits the ability of state to develop it beyond establishing the essentials for a functioning international society. These debates are becoming increasingly important to the study of IR. As the international community responds to genocide in Kosovo and Rwanda, to the 'war on terror', to the trial of former heads of state charged with war crimes and crimes against humanity, the ideas of humanitarian intervention and the progressive development of international law are essential. In Chapter 8 we will return to the issue.

CONCLUSION: COMING TO TERMS WITH IR THEORY

Chapters 3 and 4 have presented only the basics of traditional IR theory. Each tradition offers many core insights into world politics yet they offer opposing world views. How do we cope with this at such an early stage of an engagement with world politics? The simple answer is to suspend judgement until you are in a much stronger position to make a decision about which set of arguments you think are the most important. For now you should simply concentrate on attaining a critical grasp of the basics of each tradition or school. This will allow you to appreciate what the studies you will come across are attempting to do and will put you in a solid position to understand what is working beneath the surface in arguments about global events and the foreign and security policy or economic policy of key actors. If you were to glance through international news today you will see governmental and journalistic opinion on a range of issues. As we write this the issues are global warming and the need to get the Kyoto protocol working fully, the war on terror, the UN approach to nuclear energy experiments in the Middle East and to the prosecution of international crimes, European Union enlargement, the rise and rise of energy costs, and the need for international intervention in Africa. If you approach these issues critically, not as an attempt to simply gather information about the facts but with a view to understanding the various positions in the debate, you will find clear examples of realist and liberal ideas. The deeper insight into the issues that we face in international politics that we gain from this is invaluable to your progress in IR.

TOPICS FOR DISCUSSION

1   What are the key differences between structural and normative liberalism?
2   What are the core values of cosmopolitan liberalism?
3   In what sense is the theory of complex interdependence a liberal theory?
4   What is the democratic peace thesis?
5   To what extent do you think the English school could forge a path between liberalism and realism?

FURTHER READING

Most textbooks have a section on liberalism or on idealism. Here we recommend you read some of the classic texts that form the core of the debates. As a starting point you should read the short essay by Kant that forms a touchstone for much normative liberalism:

Kant, I. (1983 [1795]) *Perpetual Peace*, trans. T. Humphrey, Indianapolis, IN: Hackett.

A specialist textbook will help here, for example:

Boucher, D. (1998) *Political Theories of International Relations from Thucydides to The Present*, Oxford: Oxford University Press.

ON DEMOCRATIC PEACE THESIS

Doyle, M. (1983a) 'Kant, Liberal Legacies and Foreign Affairs', *Philosophy and Public Affairs* 12 (3): 205–235.

Doyle, M. (1983b) 'Kant, Liberal Legacies and Foreign Affairs Part 2', *Philosophy and Public Affairs* 12 (4): 323–353.

ON LIBERAL INTERNATIONALISM

Keohane, R. and Nye, J. (1977) *Power and Interdependence: World Politics in Transition*, Boston, MA: Little, Brown.

Keohane, R. (1988) 'International Institutions: Two Approaches', *International Studies Quarterly* 32 (4): 379–396.

ON CONTEMPORARY COSMOPOLITANISM

Kant, I. (1983 [1795]) *Perpetual Peace*, trans. T. Humphrey, Indianapolis, IN: Hackett.

O'Neill, O. (1991) 'Transnational Justice', in D. Held (ed.) *Political Theory Today*, Cambridge: Polity Press.

Pogge, T. (2002) *World Poverty and Human Rights: Cosmopolitan Responsibilities and Reforms*, Cambridge: Polity Press.

ON THE ENGLISH SCHOOL

Bull, H. (1969) 'International Theory: The Case for a Classical Approach', in K. Knorr and J.N. Rosenau (eds) *Contending Approaches to International Politics*, Princeton: Princeton University Press, pp. 20–38.

Buzan, B. (2001) 'The English School: An Underexploited Resource in IR', *Review of International Studies* 27: 471–488.

5

CHALLENGING ANARCHY

Building world politics

In Chapters 1 to 4 of this book we have introduced you to the theoretical origins of IR as a discipline and suggested that one perspective in IR, realism, has become the dominant paradigm for the study of IR both within academia (universities) and within the more policy-oriented work of defence analysts, military tacticians and foreign policy makers. Realism, in many ways, appears to be such a straightforward view of international politics. It accords closely to the world of inter-state rivalries that dominate the international pages of the newspapers and the TV news. However, one of the major criticisms of realism has been that it is a state-centric theory that overlooks the role that a whole range of different organizations play in challenging the existence of anarchy. Thus much of this chapter will focus on the growing importance to the study of IR of a range of so-called 'non-state actors' or 'transnational actors' such as multinational firms or non-governmental organizations. These organizations have become increasingly influential in world politics and their presence often serves to bring new issues onto the agenda of international politics – economic and trade issues, environmental issues, human rights issues and many, many others. Moreover, often the appearance of these issues on the agenda of international politics has resulted in a blurring of the traditional distinction between international and domestic politics (so-called 'high' and 'low' politics).

This exploration of the role of non-state actors in international relations helps to consolidate the critique of realism that was developed in earlier chapters. As we saw, the assumption that states have always existed and that these states are sovereign, territorially bounded, rational actors, is an ideal that has rarely existed. States have never been the principal and only units of political organization, they rarely have complete control over their territories, and, as we saw in Chapter 4, the notion of rational-action is subject to so many qualifying factors that it is almost useless as a concept with any analytical value.

The term 'non-state actor' is generally utilized as a catch-all term for the plethora of different organizations currently active within world politics. However, the term non-state actor can, at times, lead to confusion. Certain organizations may not be especially independent from states, while intergovernmental organizations – organizations such as the United Nations for example – have a membership made up of states and aim to regulate the relations between states in some way. Some would suggest for example, that organizations that are comprised of a membership of states (like the UN or the European Union) should be called *supra*national organizations – because states are still the building blocks on which these institutions rest. Another problem with the term non-state actor is that it implies that states are dominant and that other actors are secondary, thus replicating the realist position that states are the dominant actors in world politics. Willetts (2005: 427) has suggested that it is perhaps more useful to employ the term 'transnational actor' to describe the various non-state groups and organizations that have an important global political role. Looking beyond the state and recognising the many different actors and interest groups that make up the complex web of relationships that take place at a global level enables us to recognise how the *trans*national nature of many of the actors in IR is in itself a challenge to the idea of *inter*national (state-centric) politics.

However, even the use of the term transnational actor is not straightforward because as we shall see in this chapter certain organizations are regionally specific (for example the European Union or the Association of South East Asian Nations) and others, such as some non-governmental organizations are essentially domestic organizations that are linked to transnational spaces through networks of activism. Rather than worrying too much about the terminology, therefore, we would suggest that the main points to be gained from this chapter are first, an understanding of the complexity of interactions between a whole range of different actors in international politics, and second, an understanding that the interactions between all of these different actors are *political* interactions – they are contributing to new understandings of where power and authority lies in the world today.

INTERNATIONAL ORGANIZATIONS

International relations has long been concerned with the role of inter-governmental organizations – viewing these organizations, made up of states, as part of the arena of international politics or 'high politics'. Debates about the role of intergovernmental organizations in world politics have their origins in the early twentieth century IR theory of the idealists who saw a specific role for them in preserving peaceful relations between states. One of the most famous idealist thinkers was the US President Woodrow Wilson who, following the carnage of the First World War, argued for the establishment of a 'League of Nations' that would act as a check on the power of aggressive and militaristic states. We provide you with a quotation from Wilson's famous 'Fourteen Points' speech in Box 5.1. Wilson believed that an organization that represented the interests of all states would act to legitimize a commitment to collective security (states working together to ensure the maintenance of peaceful international relations). The League of Nations is often presented as a failure because of its inaction in the face of the rise of Fascism in the 1930s. However, the commitment to multilateral international organizations was strengthened with the establishment of the United Nations in 1944. The UN was set up as an organization that would help to preserve peace after the end of the Second World War. The UN was to be made up of a membership of all the states of the world – thus underlining a commitment to the idea of *multilateralism* – all states working together through international organizations and abiding

BOX 5.1 MULTILATERALISM AND INTERNATIONAL ORGANIZATIONS

(a) **Wilson's Fourteenth Point (from his Fourteen Points speech, made 8 January 1918**

A general association of nations must be formed under specific covenants for the purpose of affording mutual guarantees of political independence and territorial integrity to great and small states alike.

Source: available at
http://www.yale.edu/lawweb/avalon/wilson14.htm

(b) **Article 1 of the Charter of the United Nations (signed on 26 June 1945)**

The Purposes of the United Nations are:

1 To maintain international peace and security, and to that end: to take effective collective measures for the prevention and removal of threats to the peace, and for the suppression of acts of aggression or other breaches of the peace, and to bring about by peaceful means, and in conformity with the principles of justice and international law, adjustment or settlement of international disputes or situations which might lead to a breach of the peace;

2 To develop friendly relations among nations based on respect for the principle of equal rights and selfdetermination of peoples, and to take other appropriate measures to strengthen universal peace;

3 To achieve international cooperation in solving international problems of an economic, social, cultural, or humanitarian character, and in promoting and encouraging respect for human rights and for fundamental freedoms for all without distinction as to race, sex, language, or religion; and

4 To be a center for harmonizing the actions of nations in the attainment of these common ends

Source: Charter of the United Nations, available at http://www.un.org/aboutun/charter

by the rules/laws of international politics to come up with common solutions. Multilateralism is a powerful and influential idea and was central to the establishment of both the League of Nations and the United Nations as can be seen from the quotations from Wilson and the UN Charter presented in Box 5.1.

Every member state of the UN has a vote within its representative assembly – the General Assembly. However, it is the UN's Security Council where the real power of the organization lies. The Security Council reflects the unequal power relations that exist between states – with some of the most powerful nations in the world (or at least nations that were powerful following the Allied victory in the Second World War) having permanent seats on the Security Council. These are Russia, France, the USA, the UK and China and as permanent members they have the authority to veto decisions. The Security Council is the only arm of the United Nations that has the power to make decisions that are binding on all UN member states (under the terms of the UN Charter). Decisions made by the Security Council are known as Security Council resolutions. Examples of Security Council resolutions include Resolution 1441, which called on Iraq to 'comply with its disarmament obligations' in the run-up to the Iraq War (which, controversially, was *not* sanctioned by a UN Security Council resolution). Other resolutions include Resolution 794 (1992), which authorized military intervention in Somalia in support of humanitarian relief operations, and 1325 (2000), which called on states to recognise the significant role that women can play in peacekeeping and post-conflict societies.

However, the UN not only is concerned with issues of peace and security, but also plays an important role in economic and social issues through the Economic and Social Council (ECOSOC). Have a look at the webpages of the United Nations (www.un.org) to see just how many different bodies and agencies come under the umbrella of ECOSOC. There are a number of different UN organizations involved in socio-economic issues such as the United Nations Development Programme (UNDP), the World Food Programme (WFP), United Nations High Commission for Refugees (UNHCR) and the United Nations Children's Fund (UNICEF). These organizations are directly funded by the UN and also by voluntary contributions. There are also several specialized agencies that are part of the 'UN system' but have varying degrees of separateness from ECOSOC. Indeed, many of these organizations would be considered only nominally part of the UN system. For example, they might control their own budgets, raise their own funds and run their own programmes. These specialized agencies include the World Bank and the International Monetary Fund (IMF) as well as the International Labour Organization (ILO) and the World Health Organization (WHO).

The important role that international organizations play in global economic affairs is also witnessed in the existence of three massively influential organizations. Alongside the establishment of the UN, in the 1940s an array of economic institutions were established to effectively govern the global economy – the World Bank, the IMF and the GATT which, in 1995, became the World Trade Organization. These organizations are discussed in more detail in Chapters 7 and 8, but they are collectively known as the 'Bretton Woods' institutions after the 1944 conference in New Hampshire, where they were first established. A liberal-informed perspective on the Bretton Woods institutions suggests that these are organizations that have aided the development of a multilateral framework of rules for the governance of the global economy. In this sense, therefore, the emergence of powerful multilateral financial institutions such as these is conceptualized in terms of a reconfiguration of power and authority in global politics – part of a system of global governance (a term that we return to discuss later in this chapter).

Realists, however, would suggest that the existence of international organizations like the UN and the WTO does little to challenge their view of world politics – powerful states are only ever likely to abide by UN resolutions or WTO trade rules when it suits them. Most famously the decision by the United States to invade Iraq in 2003 was an act that went against UN procedures. But we can also point to other examples such as the way in which the member states of the European Union have avoided adhering to WTO rules regarding the liberalization of agriculture. Furthermore, decision-making power within the UN resides with a small group of states (the permanent members of the Security Council), and many of the Bretton Woods institutions are dominated by the interests of rich states. At the World Bank, for example, the voting power of states is proportional to the funds that they contribute to the organization. A common criticism made of the Bretton Woods institutions is that they are organizations that are used by the rich industrialized states to control poorer countries in the Global South, forcing them to adopt certain economic and social policies in return for financial assistance. Thus realists would suggest that despite the rhetoric of multilateralism, the same old conflicts between states continue behind an internationalist façade. But despite these realist concerns, it is important to point out that the very existence of international organizations challenges the way in which we think about world politics – many states are committed to multilateralism and it remains a powerful and important concept that cannot be ignored when discussing international relations today.

REGIONAL ORGANIZATIONS

One particular type of international organization that is of considerable interest to international relations scholars in recent years has been the emergence of organizations committed to regional integration. Often these organizations take the form of free trade areas whereby states within a particular region agree to drop certain trade and investment barriers that they have in place against each other. Regional integration schemes may also be accompanied by easing the restrictions on individuals to work in other states in the region, the emergence of a common currency, common political institutions and even common policies on security and foreign policy. The EU is perhaps the best known and well established regional organization – displaying almost all of the above characteristics to varying extents. There are also whole arrays of other regional organizations of which ASEAN (the Association of Southeast Asian Nations), MERCOSUR (Mercado Común del Sur, a trading zone between Brazil, Uraguay, Argentina, Venezuela and Paraguay) and NAFTA (North American Free Trade Area) are just a few.

One of the areas of debate relating to regionalism concerns the way in which regional forms of governance and organization are challenging conventional understandings of power and authority in international politics. For example, the idea of multilevel governance (Marks and Hooghe 1996) has been introduced to encapsulate the blurring of sovereignty that has occurred in spaces such as the European Union. The notion of multilevel governance is particularly pertinent in discussing how within certain polities such as the United Kingdom there has been a devolution of political authority to subnational or subregional levels (in Wales and Scotland) taking place alongside the growing power and influence of regional forms of governance at the European level.

Increasingly, there has also emerged an interest in the security and foreign policy dimensions of regional organizations. Quite often this literature considers the extent to which regional organizations are capable of collective decision-making – for example is it possible for the European Union to have a common security policy in the same way that it has a common agricultural policy? One suggestion has been to draw upon social constructivist understandings of international politics to suggest that collective security agendas are likely to emerge in regional contexts because of the way in which norms and ideas can be used to build regional identities. This is an idea that we explore in more detail in the case study of ASEAN presented in Box 5.2.

NON-GOVERNMENTAL ORGANIZATIONS

While the significance (or insignificance) of intergovernmental organizations has been recognised and debated within IR since the early twentieth century, the significance attached to the study of transnational actors that are independent of states is perhaps a more recent phenomenon. NGO is an acronym that stands for 'non-governmental organizations' and, nowadays, NGOs are active around issues as diverse as rainforest deforestation and pollution, religious activities, humanitarian intervention in times of war and natural disaster, international human rights, and international sporting and cultural events. Operating in virtually every part of the globe, NGOs are more than mere pressure groups seeking to influence domestic politics, they have a role to play in global politics – either because they engage with issues that are of global importance, are large organizations that operate across a range of different countries, or are part of a global network of locally based organizations campaigning on issues of global significance (Salamon 1994).

BOX 5.2 ASEAN: BUILDING REGIONAL COOPERATION AND COMMUNITY

ASEAN, the Association of South East Asian Nations, was established in 1967 by the states of Indonesia, Malaysia, Philippines, Singapore and Thailand. It has subsequently developed into one of the strongest and most effective regional organizations in the developing world. This original group of five was joined by Brunei (1984) and, following the end of the Cold War, by Vietnam (1995), Laos (1997), Myanmar (1997) and Cambodia (1999). The organization was initially established to have a limited political role, a forum for the discussion of common issues and problems. The organization subsequently sought to develop into a regional economic integration scheme. In 1991, the ASEAN states agreed to establish the ASEAN Free Trade Area (AFTA) and the organization has gradually moved towards this goal.

ASEAN is more than simply a regional economic integration scheme: it has evolved into an influential actor in international politics. For example, ASEAN has proven to be very effective within a broader international forum – the Asia Pacific Economic Cooperation forum (APEC). APEC is an organization that includes a wide membership of states from around the Pacific Rim. ASEAN ensured that APEC ministerial meetings were held in an ASEAN member state every second year. Because host states are able to set the agenda of APEC meetings, this has given ASEAN a considerable degree of influence within APEC, countering the interests of the most powerful APEC member states – notably the United States and Japan. The organization has also come to play a significant role in security issues at a regional level. In 1994, the post Cold War security framework for the region was discussed at the ASEAN Regional Forum (ARF), which brought together eighteen states including Russia, China, Japan, the EU and the United States. This was important because it meant that ASEAN was able to effectively control the agenda concerning regional security issues rather than have the discussions dominated by China and the United States (Stubbs 2004).

One of the reasons why ASEAN is so interesting to consider in the context of this chapter is because its existence has played a role in the reshaping of member state's perceptions of their 'national interest' and their ways of conducting foreign policy. An issue that is often discussed in relation to ASEAN is the way in which the organization has developed its own unique culture governing relations between member states. This is often referred to as the 'ASEAN Way' (Acharya 2001). The argument is made that ASEAN has fostered a peaceful, stable and constructive relationship between its members due to a number of different factors. First, there is a commitment among all of the member states to non-interference in each other's internal affairs. Although this feature of the ASEAN Way sounds very much like traditional realism it is important to recognise that it is in fact somewhat different. What these states are doing is agreeing together within a multilateral forum to respect one another's sovereignty. This is a different idea, therefore, from the realist notion that sovereignty is something that states can properly defend only through force or the threat of force. Second, member states have placed importance on decision-making by consensus at the regional level. Leaders have often explained this commitment to consensus building by drawing upon uniquely Southeast Asian cultural ideas – in this case ideas rooted in Javanese village society which empha- size trust and mutual obligation rather than confrontation (for example, ASEAN members have ruled out the use of force against one another) (Narine 2002). But consensus building is also a reflection of the close personal ties and interrelationships between political leaders and senior bureaucrats in the region. Disputes between leaders are rarely witnessed in public and the organization has adopted a very practically minded approach to decision-making whereby leaders agree broad general frameworks and gradually work towards the establishment of firm treaties or institutions. It has therefore been suggested that ASEAN has evolved into an organization with a unique regional identity and this has strengthened its position in international affairs. The example of ASEAN is often employed to point to the limitations of realist perspectives in IR – replacing an overwhelming emphasis on the state and the 'national interest' with a focus on regional identities as the basis for collective decision-making (Eaton and Stubbs 2006).

Generally only the largest and richest NGOs are able to engage in action outside of their boundaries – these include organizations such as Greenpeace, Amnesty International, the Red Cross and ˚Médicins Sans Frontières. These large globally organized NGOs are often referred to as international non-governmental organizations. Taking an example of one of these powerful INGOs, Greenpeace (the organization involved in campaigns to protect the environment) we will now show some of the ways in which this influential INGO has been active in global politics. In particular, we will focus on the extent to which the emergence of such INGOs challenges the realist view that states remain the most important actors in world politics.

Campaigns run by Greenpeace often involve direct action to protect the environment and to draw attention to the potentially environmentally damaging practices of both states and corporations. Like many NGOs, Greenpeace relies upon the technique of 'shaming' governments with poor environmental records. The success with which Greenpeace has been able to employ such tactics demonstrates how power and influence in world politics stem not only from military capabilities or economic wealth but also from the 'moral authority' of certain actors. States are often very concerned with the impact of the activities of NGOs such as Greenpeace. This was most clearly illustrated when in 1985 the French secret service planted two bombs on the Greenpeace ship *Rainbow Warrior*, sinking it. The French government ultimately had to pay out US $8.16 million in compensation to Greenpeace. In fact the Greenpeace case also points to something very significant in contemporary world politics – how NGOs have become incredibly important actors in the area of international environmental politics; challenging the idea that international political activity is a 'state only' arena (Raustiala 1997; Newell 2006).

The influence of NGOs in world politics is also witnessed in their recognition by intergovernmental organizations. Article 71 of the charter of the United Nations empowered the Economic and Social Council of the UN to grant NGOs a 'consultative status' on various issues. Greenpeace, for example, has had consultative status in the UN body entrusted with governing international shipping, the International Maritime Organization, since 1991 (although there have been attempts by member states of the International Maritime

Organization to have Greenpeace's consultative status revoked). The World Bank has also increasingly come to recognise the importance of incorporating (often rather critical) NGO voices into its activities – although it has not gone so far as ECOSOC in this regard and critics have voiced concerns about the lack of accountability within the World Bank and IMF structures (Woods 2001).

Not only have NGOs grown in influence in recent years, but also the sheer number of NGOs has increased quite rapidly. This is due to a number of factors. First, the democratization of a number of states across the world since the end of the Cold War has created a more hospitable space for NGOs that may well not have been tolerated by authoritarian regimes. Second, many states are very weak and have come to rely increasingly on NGOs to perform tasks that would previously have been done by the state. This is often the case when states are facing major humanitarian and economic catastrophes. For example, in many sub-Saharan African states NGOs perform crucial health and social services in communities affected by the HIV/AIDs epidemic. Furthermore, states in the developing world have often been compelled to cut welfare and social spending in order to repay foreign debts and NGOs have stepped in to assume responsibility for certain social and welfare roles. Third, both the growth and increased influence of the NGOs sector is related to technological changes – in particular the advances in communications technologies. The Internet has made available to many smaller NGOs a means of communicating and networking with other organizations in other parts of the world that share common cause with them and getting their message across to a wider audience. Vast networks of alliances between various NGOs have emerged in recent decades. An example of this are the activities of the various different groups engaged in the campaigns to stop 'sweatshop' working conditions in the global clothing industry (Connor 2004). Groups campaigning around this issue include consumer associations, fair trade pressure groups, religious groups, international development organizations, trade unions in both the rich and poor countries of the world, women's groups among others. Another example of this kind of networking among social movements can be seen in the coming together of many different women's groups and activists in campaigns to have the issue of violence against women recognised as a human rights issue. Women's groups very successfully coordinated their campaigns and managed to highlight the issue at numerous UN forums and meetings throughout the 1990s (Bunch 1995; Merry 2006).

The formation of these kinds of networks are becoming increasingly common and the phrase *global civil society* is often used to sum up these diverse processes. We will return to look at some of these social movements/NGOs when we explore the emergence of the so-called 'anti-globalization' movement in Chapter 7.

The examples given above – of Greenpeace and of the campaigns around sweatshop production – are significant for another reason too. They have brought issues that are beyond the remit of 'traditional' IR onto the agenda. Campaigns around global environmental issues or labour rights in the global economy have played a role in expanding and challenging the boundaries of the discipline. We are forced to rethink the way in which IR has been characterized in realist terms as the struggle for power and wealth between competing nation-states. These new concerns are also notable in that they have an important normative dimension – they challenge us to think about what kind of world we want to live in. Furthermore, these are issues that force us to confront the artificiality of the distinction between 'international' and 'domestic' politics. After all, things like international production and labour issues and global environmental issues involve a complex interplay of actors and issues that are located both inside and outside of a state's boundaries. Environmental organizations often ask us to 'think locally and act globally' – such a phrase neatly conveys the way in which a sole focus on the 'international' is now increasingly insufficient in understanding IR.

MULTINATIONAL CORPORATIONS

One of the most significant and long recognised non-state actor in international politics is the multinational corporation. MNCs are companies that own operations (factories, offices etc.) in parts of the world outside of the state in which it was originally established. These overseas parts of the company are referred to as its subsidiaries. MNCs have been a feature of the global economy for centuries – oil companies for example, have long been organized on a multinational basis and have long been important players in global politics.

But it was with the growth of a global manufacturing sector from the 1960s onwards, as firms expanded overseas in order to seek out new sources of low cost labour in the developing world, that saw the most rapid growth in the numbers of MNCs (Held *et al.* 1999).

It is widely recognised that MNCs are economically powerful and it has become somewhat standard practice in the literature to compare the annual turnover of many large MNCs to the annual gross domestic product (GDP) of states. However, as Held *et al.* (1999) point out, a simple comparison of this nature does not tell us all that much about the complex interrelationships between states and multinational capital. MNCs use their economic power in different ways to bargain with states (and also with each other). Some have suggested that MNCs have been able to force states in the developing world to lower their labour standards, or curtail trade union rights, in a bid to secure inward investment from the firm. Others have pointed to the ways in which MNCs have considerable lobbying power – influencing government policies towards things like climate change, genetically modified foods or even decisions concerning whether or not to go to war. But at the same time, we need to recognise that the power of MNCs often stems from the fact that states have enabled corporations to go global by deregulating their economies and competing to attract foreign direct investment.

Stopford and Strange (1991: 2) argue that the relation between states and firms has taken on a 'triangular' character. Diplomacy in the world today occurs at three different intersections illustrated in Figure 5.1. First, there are the 'traditional' diplomatic inter-actions between states – things like trade negotiations, bilateral treaties, decisions to go to war or attempts to try to avoid war. These traditional inter-state interactions remain an important component in the international political scene (importantly the point here is *not* that states are no longer important actors in international politics, they are just no longer the *only* important actors). Second, we can point to relations between states and firms. For example, firms might lobby state governments to take a particular course of action or states might seek ways to restrict the activities of MNCs or might undertake things like taxation reform or restrictions on trade union activities as a means of attracting foreign direct investment (when MNCs set up subsidiaries in other states). Finally, the growing significance of

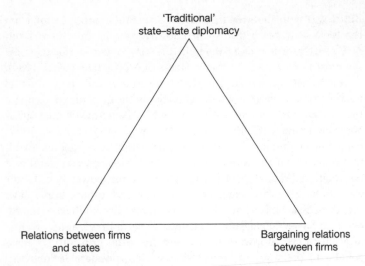

Figure 5.1 Stopford and Strange on triangular diplomacy

corporate mergers and alliances between MNCs also means that even relationships solely between firms have important global political consequences. What is really significant about their model of triangular diplomacy is that they view all three of these interrelationships as *political*. In other words, even the negotiations between MNCs (for example over a corporate merger or alliance) have important political consequences for the world that we live in today, and are just as important a topic for scholars of IR as the diplomatic bargaining that goes on between states.

PRIVATE POWER AND AUTHORITY: LOOKING BEYOND THE MNC

It has been argued that the increased power and influence of MNCs in IR is a reflection of the increasing privatization of authority in international politics today. This is the idea that states have actually given up some of their power to a whole range of economically powerful non-state actors – in particular firms. One example of this is the emergence of something called private military companies (PMCs) that provide trained security and military personnel to states

(Shearer 1998). The use of PMCs is generally associated with weak conflict-ridden states in the poorest parts of the world – for example PMCs have been associated with the conflicts in Sierra Leone and Papua New Guinea. But PMCs have also been put to extensive use by the United States, with the Iraq occupation characterized by an increased use of subcontracting of military work to private companies.

In investigating the role of the private sector in international politics, it is also important to note that two of the world's most profitable industries – illegal weapons and drugs – are largely controlled by groups of non-legitimate international private actors. The scope and effectiveness of organized criminal activities increased enormously over the course of the twentieth century. It is now possible to talk of organized crime as being 'transnational' in character. There exist a vast number of criminal organizations – some of the largest and best known include Italian organized crime groups such as the Cosa Nostra of Sicilly and the Neapolitan Camorra, the Japanese boroyokudan, the Chinese Triads, the South East Asian and Latin American drug cartels and the emergence of the 'Russian mafiya' (often not Russian at all but Georgian, Ukrainian and Chechnyan).

What these criminal organizations share with the NGOs and firms already discussed in this chapter is that they are also going global – becoming transnational actors. Organized criminal activities have often followed ethnic diasporas as they move overseas, but they have sought out allies overseas. Galeotti (2001) therefore argues that criminal organizations have often come to take on some of the characteristics of MNCs, 'mirroring legitimate business in its increasingly global outlook and trend towards multinationalism' (Galeotti 2001: 208).

INTERNATIONAL TERRORIST ORGANIZATIONS

Discussions of non-legitimate actors in international relations are incomplete without mentioning terrorist organizations. Violent political action against civilian targets has long been a feature of both domestic and international politics. Yet it is with the terrorist attacks of 11 September 2001 that the study of global terrorist organizations has moved up the agenda of IR. The events of 9/11 demonstrated to the world that world politics wasn't simply about conflicts between states – that an organization like al-Qaeda could inflict as much, in fact maybe even more damage, on the most economically and militarily powerful state in the world than any 'enemy state'. Al-Qaeda is often referred to as an international or global terrorist organization. One reason for this is the way in which terrorism is viewed as increasingly 'globalized' (Cronin 2002); the organization is perceived as a global network operating across national boundaries and making use of modern information communication technologies. Al-Qaeda is also regarded as a globally focused international terrorist organization in terms of its objectives. Whereas many terrorist groups have worked within an understanding of international politics whereby the state is the most important actor – for example groups such as ETA in Spain are secessionist groups that seek to establish their own states – global terrorist groups are perceived to be challenging the whole viability of an international system based around the existence of states. Of course, al-Qaeda is not the first terrorist organization to have these more globally focused aims and objectives – we could point to communist and anarchist terrorist organizations during the nineteenth and twentieth centuries espousing similar ideas (Jensen 2001).

One of the problems for the student of IR when it comes to the issue of terrorism is that often it is very difficult to accurately define what a terrorist organization actually is (is a terrorist any different from a freedom fighter?) (Chomsky 2002). More fundamentally, some would argue that states themselves can engage in acts of terrorism – assassinations, acts of mass murder, hijackings, bombings, kidnapping and violent intimidation have all been carried out by states. States also play an important role in supporting terrorist organizations thus blurring the line between the state and the non-state actors (Byman 2005). So essentially we can see that looking at terrorist organizations in IR raises several questions about the role of the state in international politics that cannot adequately be dealt with within the realist frame.

CHALLENGING STATE CENTRICISM: RECONCEPTUALIZING WORLD POLITICS

Reflecting on the overview of all of the different transnational actors surveyed in this chapter, let us turn now to think more closely about how the emergence of these global actors confronts and undermines the realist vision of world politics. First, there is the rather obvious point that the emergence of all of these different actors presents a challenge to the view that the state is the most important actor in world politics. Second, while many organizations may not have the same kinds of power and resources as states, they do challenge the notion of state-sovereignty (the principle that establishes the nation-state as an independent actor with supreme political authority within the international system) because their activities easily cross state boundaries and often because of this easily escape state control. For example, a state may wish to regulate the activities of a MNC operating within its borders that is polluting the local environment but worries that if it puts pressure on the MNC it will simply move to another state in which environmental regulation is much more lax. Another example might be that a state wants to crack down on activities of criminal gangs but finds that it is almost impossible to track the business activities of these gangs because of the way in which criminal finances are 'laundered' through off-shore banking centres. Finally, it could also be claimed that the development of vast networks of interrelationships in global politics and the emergence of new centres of authority and power beyond the state presents a challenge not only to ideas of world politics being made up of sovereign states, but also challenges that notion of anarchy that is so fundamental to realist analysis.

In Figure 5.2, for example, we present two quite different pictures of the international system. On the left we see the realist view, in which IR is made up only of sovereign states (and these states collide against one another like 'billiard balls'). In the right-hand side of the diagram we present a quite different picture in which IR is made up of a range of different actors and these actors operate inside and outside of the state. Thinking about the world in terms of networks of interconnected actors allows for a rather more sophisticated understanding of the world than the colliding billiard balls of realism (Risse-Kapen 1995; Dicken *et al.* 2001).

What we have seen in this chapter is that there are a complex range of actors in world politics. But how might we try to reconceptualize world politics to take account of all of these different actors? We have already come across some concepts that introduce new ways

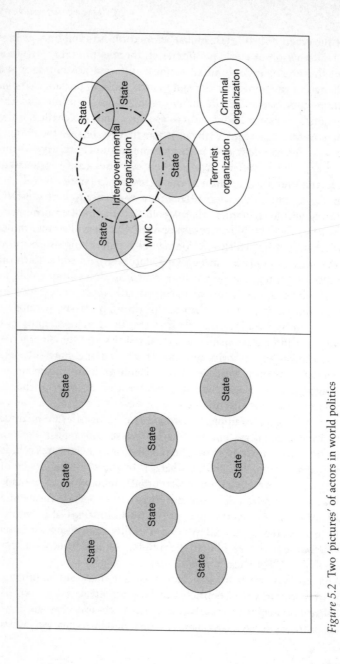

Figure 5.2 Two 'pictures' of actors in world politics

of thinking about international politics – for example multilevel governance and triangular diplomacy. We now turn to look at some of the more general ways of conceptualizing an international politics made up of multiple and varied actors.

COMPLEX INTERDEPENDENCY AND THINKING ABOUT INSTITUTIONS

The discussion of non-state actors in international politics can be seen in the early work of the *neo-liberal institutionalists* such as Robert Keohane and Joseph Nye (see Chapter 4). In the early 1970s Keohane and Nye (1971) introduced ideas of 'transnational relations' that stressed the important role that non-state actors were increasingly taking in international affairs. These writings were produced during a period of international history in which a *détente*, or thawing of relations, between the major protagonists in the Cold War (the USA and the USSR) was taking place. By the late 1970s however, as the Cold War heated up, there was a re-emphasis on more realist state-centric ways of thinking about international politics. Yet importantly, the work of these neo-liberal institutionalists was never completely at odds with more state-centric theories. This is because they conceded that while a range of non-state transnational actors had emerged, the state remained the most important actor in international politics. Transnational actors mattered because they played a role in mitigating anarchy – they contributed to the creation of an international political environment characterized by 'complex interdependency' between a range of state and non-state actors, which, it was argued would contribute to the ability of states to cooperate (what was termed 'cooperation under anarchy'). The significance that Keohane attached to international institutions in fostering cooperation is discussed in the quotation presented in Box 5.3.

In his book *International Institutions and State Power* Keohane (1989a) spelt out his idea that world politics is institutionalized – and that it is this institutionalization that better enables the prospects for states to cooperate with one another. Keohane outlines three different types of institution. The first are formal institutions. These formal institutions are not just intergovernmental organizations like the UN or ASEAN, this category also include a wide variety of

BOX 5.3 ROBERT KEOHANE ON THE IMPORTANCE OF INTERNATIONAL INSTITUTIONS

I believe that international institutions are worth studying because they are pervasive and important in world politics and because their operation and evolution are difficult to understand. But I also urge attention to them on normative grounds. International institutions have the *potential* to facilitate cooperation, and without international cooperation I believe that the prospects for our species will be very poor indeed. Cooperation is not always benign; but without cooperation, we will be lost. Without institutions there will be little cooperation. And without knowledge of how institutions work – and what makes them work well – there are likely to be fewer, and worse, institutions than if such knowledge is widespread.

Robert Keohane, *International Institutions and State Power* (1989a: 174, original emphasis)

transnational actors such as NGOs and MNCs. The second group of institutions are what Keohane labels regimes. Regimes are essentially the embodiment of issue-specific international problem solving whereby a range of state and non-state actors come together around issues such as nuclear proliferation, international trade or climate change. Finally, Keohane argues that conventions (ways of doing things) also have an institutional quality – thus for Keohane the convention of reciprocity in international affairs (that one state can always expect to be treated in a manner commensurate with its own actions) has an institutionalized quality. The argument is made that these conventions are essential building blocks in the foundation of formal institutions and regimes.

THE IDEA OF NEW MEDIEVALISM

While Keohane provides us with a descriptive classification of a range of different actors, he remained committed to the idea that the state was still the more important actor in international politics. In this sense, Keohane's typology is somewhat limited in the extent to which it can really analyse the changing nature of the international political landscape. Other perspectives have therefore sought to try and encapsulate the extent to which power is being reconfigured in world politics today. What these perspectives suggest is that power is not something that we should associate only with states. In the 1970s the English school scholar Hedley Bull started to think through this problem and presented a number of different scenarios for how international politics might evolve. One of these he labelled new medievalism – the view that world politics may be coming to resemble the non-territorial and overlapping organization of (political) authority in medieval times (Bull 1977: 254–255). In the medieval period this would have been things like the authority of the Church (a non-state actor), and the existence of overlapping principalities, empires and city states. So the neo-medieval position suggests that the world is coming to resemble that state of affairs with international organizations, regional organizations, global civil society, and local and regional governments exercising authority over different issues.

Bull pointed our attention to a number of features of international politics that could evolve to change the world from one in which power and authority lay principally with states to one in which there were multiple and overlapping sources of power and authority. First, he pointed to the regional integration of some states (notably those within Europe) and the fragmentation or disintegration of some states as a result of secessionism (Bull 1977: 264–268). Bull was particularly interested in cases where secessionism does not lead to the creation of new states – so the devolution of political authority that has occurred within the UK in Wales and Scotland would be a good example of this.

Second, a revival in private international violence is presented as a challenge to the power and authority of the state (Bull 1977: 268–270). Bull specifically pointed to the rise of terrorist groups. However, it is the rise of private military companies that creates an even greater challenge to the authority of the state. This is because classical definitions of the state claim that states have complete authority over the legitimate use of violence in both the domestic and international sphere. Thus what we can see here is the ceding of this fundamental aspect of a state's sovereignty to private non-state actors.

Third, Bull pointed to the growth of transnational corporations, and fourth, to the role of technology in unifying the world (and thereby undermining ideas that we live in separate territorially defined state units). So what he presents to us is a picture of world politics which is fundamentally at odds with the realist vision of state-centric IR. When Bull presented these ideas in the 1970s they were viewed as one possible scenario (and one that he felt would not bring much stability to international politics and was therefore an unlikely future). However, in recent years these ideas have been popularized considerably (Linklater 1998; Freiderichs 2001). This is hardly surprising; the above trends that Bull noted have all become increasingly important and significant to our understanding of global politics today.

GLOBAL GOVERNANCE

The ideas of complex interdependency and new medievalism are often seen as key conceptual ideas in the emergence of an important field of study within IR – that of global governance. The concept of global governance is often employed to encapsulate the many different layers of authority that exist in an increasingly complex world (Rosenau 1995). However, global governance is also a rather loose term that means quite distinct things to different groups of people. Indeed, like globalization (a concept that we discuss in more detail in Chapter 7) we would suggest that the global governance is an essentially contested concept.

For many scholars, global governance is a concept that is employed mainly in terms of the need to reform and expand the powers of intergovernmental organizations in an increasingly globalized and complex world facing multiple threats to global order. To others, the concept is employed to look at the way in which a complex interplay of state, intergovernmental and non-state actors have come together to deal with problems of global significance. Robert Keohane's work is particularly influential for this group of scholars not only because he introduces ideas of complex interdependency and cooperation under anarchy – but also because, as we saw in Box 5.3, Keohane is committed to the idea that cooperation brings positive results. In both of these cases then, global governance is seen as a good and positive step – a reconfiguration of power and authority in world politics that can play a role in helping the peoples of the world come up with solutions to a diverse range of global problems (such as 'Third World' debt, global poverty and environmental degradation and climate change).

However, many scholars take a much less benign 'problem-solving' view of global governance as a concept. The critical theorist Robert Cox, for example, has employed the term 'global governance' in pointing to the way in which powerful corporate actors such as MNCs, certain governments or elements within governments, and a range of non-governmental actors are united around support for a model of 'globalization' that entrenches and protects the interests of global capitalism. Writers such as Cox leave us with the suggestion that global governance may be a useful way of understanding the reconfiguration of power and authority in world politics – but this might not necessarily be something that benefits all in the way that writers like Robert Keohane would suggest. Indeed, Cox argues that the gradual disillusionment with global capitalism within civil society could in fact be the basis upon which a radical, even revolutionary, reshaping of world politics takes place.

CONCLUSION

We have tried to introduce you to a huge array of different ideas in this chapter. We started by looking at the relationships between states and intergovernmental and regional organizations, before turning to look at the challenge to state power and authority that have come from a range of non-state actors. What this discussion should have indicated to you is that the relationship between states and non-state/intergovernmental actors is exceptionally complicated. What we are not putting forward in this chapter is an argument that the state is an insignificant actor in international politics. Indeed, the purpose of the discussion raised in the final section of this chapter was to try and present the idea that what is taking place is a reconfiguration of political power in international politics in which states continue to play a centrally important (though somewhat different) role.

One theme that can be drawn from this discussion is that you cannot meaningfully have a separate 'international' realm of politics. Realist perspectives, and neo-realist perspectives in particular, have presented us with the idea that 'the international' is a realm of international politics that differs from domestic politics because of the absence of authority (or as they term it 'anarchy'). As Robert Cox has argued, the international system should be conceptualized as a state-society complex that crosses across domestic and international levels of analysis.

TOPICS FOR DISCUSSION

1 What is multilateralism and do you think that it remains an important principle of international politics today?
2 What, in your view, are the major factors behind the increased regionalization of world politics today?
3 What new issues and debates do you think that NGOs have brought onto the international political agenda?
4 Do you think that MNCs are more powerful than states?
5 Which of the theoretical perspectives introduced so far in this book do you think offer us the best understanding of the role of non-state actors in world affairs?

FURTHER READING

GENERAL, NON-STATE ACTORS

Nicholson, M. (2002) *International Relations: A Concise Introduction*, second edition, Basingstoke: Palgrave Macmillan. See Chapter 3, 'Beyond the State: Non-State Actors in the Modern World', pp. 34–49.

Willetts, P. (2005) 'Transnational Actors and International Organisations in Global Politics' in J. Baylis and S. Smith (eds) *The Globalization of World Politics*, third edition, Oxford: Oxford University Press, pp. 425–450.

Risse-Kapen, T. (1995) *Bringing Transnational Relations Back In: Non-state Actors, Domestic Structures and International Institutions*, Cambridge: Cambridge University Press.

Keohane, R. (1989) *International Institutions and State Power: Essays in International Relations Theory*, Boulder, CO: Westview Press.

THE UNITED NATIONS

Weiss, T., Forsythe, D. and Coate, R. (2004) *The United Nations and Changing World Politics*, fourth edition, Boulder, CO: Westview Press.

REGIONALISM

Stubbs, R. and Underhill, G. (eds) (2000) *Political Economy and the Changing Global Order*, second edition, Oxford: Oxford University Press. See section 3, 'Regional dynamics', pp. 231–296.

GLOBAL CIVIL SOCIETY

Glasius, M., Kaldor, M. and Anheier, H. (eds) (2006) *Global Civil Society 2005/6*, London: Sage.

MULTINATIONAL CORPORATIONS

Stopford, J. and Strange, S. (1991) *Rival States, Rival Firms: Competition for World Market Share*, Cambridge: Cambridge University Press.

TRANSNATIONAL ORGANIZED CRIME

Galeotti, M. (2001) 'Underworld and Upperworld: Transnational Crime and Global Society', in D. Josselin and W. Walace (eds) *Non-state Actors in World Politics*, Basingstoke: Palgrave, pp. 203–217.

TERRORISM

Booth, K. and Dunne, T. (eds) (2002) *Worlds in Collision: Terror and the Future of Global Order*, Basingstoke: Palgrave MacMillan, pp. 128–137.

GLOBAL GOVERNANCE

O'Brien, R. and Williams, M. (2004) *Global Political Economy: Evolution and Dynamics*, London: Palgrave MacMillan. See Chapter 11, 'Governing the Global Political Economy'.

Wilkinson, R. (2005) *The Global Governance Reader*, London: Routledge.

6

CRITICIZING WORLD POLITICS

The development of realist IR has been accompanied by the development of a series of criticisms of *inter*national politics. We saw in Chapter 5, for example, that while realism rests upon a view of world politics in which the state is the principal actor, the reality is much messier. A variety of transnational actors interact with states, and with one another, in increasingly complex ways. Thinking about the role of transnational actors is just one of the ways in which we might come up with an alternative to realist understandings of world politics. In this chapter, we seek to expand on some of the themes that we developed in Chapter 4, showing you how different theorists of international relations have sought to come up with alternatives to realist IR.

There are a variety of different theoretical perspectives within the academic study of IR. It is useful to think of these different theories as painting quite different 'pictures' of world politics. They are all looking at the same thing, but each theorist decides to emphasize different things in their particular picture of world politics. Let us consider some of the major theories of IR that we have already covered in this book so far: realism, idealism and the English school. Although all three of these theories are concerned with understanding the nature of world politics, they all come up with quite different explanations (see Box 6.1).

BOX 6.1 COMPETING 'PICTURES' OF WORLD POLITICS

Realism   The world is made up of unitary and sovereign nation-states that operate in a competitive self-help environment (anarchy). States act rationally, in the national interest, in order to maximize power and thus ensure survival. The political interests of states (power) should always be prioritized in relations with other states and the route to power is almost always defined in terms of military capabilities. Because world politics is made up of states with competing power interests, there is a certain inevitability that states will go to war with one another.

Idealism   The individual, rather than the state, ought to be at the centre of a theory of international politics. States are, in effect, a 'necessary evil' and the existence of large, unrepresentative, undemocratic states fuels the path to war.

Individuals are rational, they are 'utility maximizers' – they wish to make things as good as possible for themselves. They therefore share a deep-rooted 'harmony of interests'. These interests include things like personal freedoms and human rights and opportunities to engage in wealth creation. States that are organized around principles of democracy and free trade enable the individual's interests to be reflected in inter-state relations. Inevitably, these democratic, economic-liberal (free trade) states are less likely to go to war with one another because this would go against the individual's 'harmony of interests'.

English school   English school followers put forward the view that states are important actors in world politics and operate under conditions of anarchy, but that they can coexist with one another within the context of a society of states. This society of states has evolved historically and refers to the various norms of international behaviour, international laws and cross-cutting interrelationships between states that shape relations between states and bring some order to international politics.

We have here three very different 'pictures' of world politics. The realist view that emphasizes the role of the state in international affairs – portraying states as power seekers operating in the 'national-interest'. In this view there is relatively little scope for discussions of ethics and morality, states simply do what they have to do in order to survive. Idealists, by contrast focus our attention on the individual, raising normative questions about how world politics ought to evolve in order to ensure that peaceful international relations prevail. Finally, the English school tried to develop a position some way between these two approaches highlighting both the sovereign nature of states and the need to think of these states as acting within a context of something that they call 'international society'.

But not only are differences between the various theories of international relations to do with the kind of picture that they paint of international politics, but also there are differences in the way that they paint their pictures – the tools and techniques that they use to portray to us their vision of the world. When looking at distinctions between theories, therefore, we also need to consider the issue of methodology, the tools and techniques that scholars use to come up with their explanations/analyses of world politics. This is an important issue because some of the most recent, and most innovative, criticisms of realism have focused on methodological questions (how realists come up with their arguments).

METHODOLOGIES IN IR

All three of the theories that are outlined above take what might be called a classical methodological approach – one that is based upon immersing oneself in the subject and coming up with careful, considered analysis based upon a deep understanding of history and philosophy (Bull 1969). During the course of the twentieth century, many theorists of IR became dissatisfied with this classical tradition in scholarship – they wanted to develop theories that were much more rigorous, that could be tested and verified just like a scientific experiment.

The gradual shift towards a more 'scientific' or *positivist* method in IR is first seen in the writings of realist scholars like Morgenthau and E.H. Carr. Morgenthau declared that politics 'is governed by objective laws that have their roots in human nature' (Morgenthau 1985 [1948]: 4). This supposes that politics is essentially a science, that the basic underlying principles of political behaviour can be discovered through the adoption of a more objective and scientific approach to the study of the social phenomena. In writing *Politics among Nations*, Morgenthau (1948) thus sought to develop a general theory of realism founded on the systematic and empirical study of international politics. However, while Morgenthau certainly endorsed a search for generalizable rules of international politics that can help us to understand the material world – his theories are generally *not* understood as a clear-cut endorsement of the kinds of positivist methodology that were championed during the so-called 'behaviouralist revolution' of the 1960s. Morgenthau's work can be associated more with a classical methodological tradition. After all, many of his assumptions relating to human nature depended more upon metaphysical assumptions about human nature and a close reading of history than a real attempt at scientific objectivity.

It was scholars like Kenneth Waltz who more clearly adopted an approach to devising theories of international relations known as positivist empiricism – being able to determine through the application of scientific principles meaningful facts about the social world that stand up to rigorous testing. Waltz was a realist, but by bringing positivist principles to bear on the subject of IR, he reworked and simplified realism, creating something we now know as neo-realism (see Chapter 3). While agreeing with Morgenthau that objectivity is required, and a scientific approach should be utilized, as a neo-realist he disputed the idea that we can base our understanding of IR on a study of human nature (Waltz 1959). Humanity, to the neo-realist, is an irrelevant side issue – we need to be able to understand the scientific 'laws' of international relations (i.e. general principles that can be discerned through a process of objective testing and verification). The wider context for these neo-realist developments was the clamour across a number of academic disciplines to develop a more scientific research programme during what became known as the behavioural revolution of the 1950s and 1960s (Jackson and Sørenson 2003: 229–233).

The neo-realist perspective was highly seductive as it offered a parsimonious (simple) theory of international relations that provided a general model to explain how world politics operated. During the Cold War era neo-realism seemed to offer an excellent explanation for the foreign policy-making decisions of both the USA and the USSR. According to the logic of neo-realism we do not need to look inside states to understand their behaviour (this is referred to a 'black box' view of the state). This black box view of the state is based on Waltz's proposition that we can 'scientifically' understand international relations only by looking at how the international structure (anarchy) impinges on the behaviour of 'units' (states). The anarchic international system generates a climate of uncertainty compelling all states to be distrustful of the intentions of other states. States will therefore seek to ensure that they have as much power as possible relative to other states. This characterization of world politics seemed to fit extremely well with the reality of the Cold War. During the Cold War there were two very different states, the USA – a liberal capitalist-democratic state – and the Communist USSR, yet both states were pursuing broadly similar foreign policies and international politics was characterized by a climate of distrust between the two states and their allies.

Of course, certain states are more capable than others in this pursuit of power. Thus in order to enhance their position in international politics relative to other states, weaker states might form alliances with other states (although the extent to which these states can ever really trust their alliance partners is limited). A variety of alliance formations exist, but neo-realists argued that a situation of bipolarity (when there are two major centres of power in the international system each of whom have forged alliances with weaker states) brings considerable stability to the international system because it involved a rough balancing-of-power to international politics. The balancing of power between the USSR and the USA during the Cold War was seen by neo-realists as bringing stability and order to international politics.

What seemed to be the case was that during the Cold War neo-realism offered the best way of understanding world politics. In fact, by the 1970s, even the more liberal influenced scholars of the day had rejected the classical philosophical methods of idealism in favour of a liberal theory of international relations that accepted the structural qualities of anarchy in shaping the behaviour of states and endorsed a scientific (positivist) method in attempting to understand world politics. The only real difference between the neo-realists and these neo-liberal institutionalists (Chapter 4) was that the latter saw a role for institutions (e.g. international organizations, treaties, established ways of conducting international relations) in mitigating the effects of the anarchic structure of world politics on state behaviour. As we saw in Chapter 1, this hegemony of a positivist position rooted in a Waltzian neo-realism led Ole Waever (1996: 163–164) to claim that the debate between neo-realists and neo-liberal institutionalists that occurred in the discipline throughout the 1970s and 1980s was little more than a 'neo-neo synthesis'. In essence this was no kind of debate at all – neo-realism had defined the parameters of intellectual discussion in international relations and all that those scholars of a more liberal persuasion could do was to make noises about the role of international institutions and norms while accepting the broader claims of the neo-realist paradigm.

However, by the 1980s a new methodological turn was taking place within the academic discipline of IR. There emerged a diverse group of scholars whose work critically engaged with the method-ological problems posed by positivism. These scholars (often collec-tively referred to as the post-positivists) asked questions such as:

- To what extent can we really ever come up with testable verifiable, empirical 'facts' about world politics. (That is, questioning the assumption of epistemological empiricism – that we see the world in terms of certain provable facts.)
- Is it really possible to create theory in a neutral scientific manner. (That is, does the theorist really create theories on the basis of scientific enquiry, or does the theorist's own social position – their class, race, gender etc. – in some way affect the way in which they see the world?)
- Do claims of value-free neutrality actually obscure the extent to which theories serve the interests of the most powerful groups within society? (That is, by claiming something as neutral are theories just prioritizing one set of preferences above another equally valid one?)

EXAMPLES OF POST-POSITIVISM

What post-positivist theories attempt to do is to present a more reflective form of theoretical inquiry. They raise epistemological questions (how is it that we come to accept particular theories as better – or closer to the 'truth' than others?), ontological questions (why is it that we accept certain categories of analysis as fixed/natural?) and normative questions (does theory have a role to play in bringing about change, raising moral/ethical questions etc.?). Post-positivism is not a coherent political position – '[i]t presents itself as a rather loosely patched-up umbrella for a confusing array of only remotely related philosophical articulations.' (Lapid 1989: 239). However, attempts have been made to draw out the broad similarities found in post-positivist scholarship (e.g. Lapid 1989). These similarities include: the rejection of grand theories of international relations rooted in a scientific commitment to objective and generalizable knowledge of the world; the concern to show how knowledge of the world is always rooted in the perspective of the theorist; a commitment to a greater plurality of methodological techniques in building a more 'reflective' theory of international politics (one in which the researcher acknowledges their subjective positioning in relationship to the material being studied). However, as Smith (2000) notes these 'reflectivist approaches tend to be more united by their opposition to realism and positivism than by any shared notion of what should replace it' (Smith, 2000: 383). Here we outline three traditions that are generally associated with the post-positivist turn in IR: critical theory, postmodernism and feminism, and a fourth, constructivism, that seeks to chart a path someway between positivism and post-positivism.

Although the emergence of positivist method (and neo-realism in particular) in the 1960s significantly altered the majority of IR scholarship, the post-positivist turn has been much less influential in terms of forcing established scholars to rethink some of their major ideas. People working in the post-positivist tradition have often been met with scepticism and cynicism, something that is observed by the IR theorist Steve Smith in Box 6.2.

BOX 6.2 STEVE SMITH CONSIDERS POST-POSITIVISM

Once established as common sense, theories become incredibly powerful since they delineate not simply what can be known but also what is sensible to talk about or suggest. Those who swim outside the safe waters risk more than simply the judgment that their theories are wrong; their entire ethical or moral stance may be ridiculed or seen as dangerous just because their theoretical assumptions are deemed unrealistic. Defining common sense is therefore the ultimate act of political power. In this sense what is at stake in debates about epistemology is very significant for political practice. Theories do not simply explain or predict, they tell us what possibilities exist for human action and intervention; they define not merely our explanatory possibilities but also our ethical and practical horizons.

Steve Smith 'Positivism and Beyond', in S. Smith,
K. Booth and M. Zawelski (eds) *International
Theory: Positivism and Beyond* (1996: 16)

CRITICAL THEORY

The work of a range of 'critical international theorists' has been highly influential in terms of bringing the concerns of ordinary people into the realm of international relations. What all critical theorists have in common is that they share a concern with emancipatory politics – bringing about fundamental changes for the least advantaged groups within society by removing hierarchical social structures. Inevitably, many critical theorists owe a debt to the work of Karl Marx, the nineteenth century philosopher/political-economist who wrote of the subordination of the working class (proletariat) in capitalist society. But theirs is also a post-positivist tradition because they raise concerns about the way in which theory is made and the ways in which powerful groups of people are able to push forward the theories that best suit their own interests.

In a 1981 article the critical theorist Robert Cox distinguished between two types of theory: 'problem solving theory' and 'critical theory'. Problem solving theory 'takes the world as it finds it' and views the purpose of theory as studying the world (as it is) in order to come up with ways of making the various institutions and social relationships that make up international politics function smoothly and effectively. By contrast, critical theory 'stands apart from the prevailing order of the world and asks how that order came about' (Cox 1981: 129). It does not accept the world as it is, but asks questions concerning how the various institutions and social relationships have come about and whether they can be transformed. Realism and neo-realism are clearly problem solving theories; they do not challenge us to think critically about how the world functions, but base their claim to legitimacy on the suggestion that they provide the most 'realistic' account of world politics. The realists' approach is also ahistorical (unchanging) – it is based on the assumption that states are the primary actors in world politics, when, as we saw in Chapters 1 and 2, the very notion of the state is a relatively recent invention.

Critical theory raises questions concerning the social construction of knowledge. This is the idea that what we accept as 'knowledge' reflects a process whereby society comes to accept certain knowledge claims as better or 'more truthful' than others. Cox famously wrote that 'theory is always *for* someone and *for* some purpose' (Cox 1981: 128, original emphasis). Thus Cox sought to challenge the assumption that the social 'scientist' can really objectively study the world in a way that their own personal interests do not pervade the work that they do. But more significantly, what Cox is arguing is that there are certain theories that come to be accepted as normal or a 'common-sense' view of politics, when in fact these are theories that act to serve the interests of the most powerful. The implication here is that we cannot ever have a politically neutral analysis of social phenomena. In fact, presenting explanations of social phenomena in neutral depoliticized terms is in itself an act of political power (Hutchings 1999). Economic analysis in particular can be criticized on these grounds. By presenting 'the economy' as a sphere separate from society that requires the application of highly technical 'scientific' theories to understand it, policy-makers are able to present economic reforms as politically neutral – when in fact the intro-duction of policies such as cutting welfare spending or curtailing the rights of trade unions (reforms that are typically justified in terms of providing economic efficiency) may well serve the interests of the powerful (and richest) groups within society.

Thinking about theories of IR, a critical theorist might also raise questions concerning how realist IR serves the interests of dominant elites. Realism is a theory of international relations that has been massively influential in foreign policy circles, and has been accepted as a 'common-sense' view of the world. However, the realist notion that great powers are needed to provide stability in the international system acts to justify the status quo, as much as it acts to explain it. Also, if the logic of realism is to suggest that all states should invest in their military capabilities – this might well suit a rich country like Britain or the USA very well, but can a state like Tanzania, crippled by international debt and one of the poorest countries in the world, really afford to pursue these kinds of policies? What needs to be asked is, do the stronger states benefit from the perpetuation of the realist 'myth' of world politics?

Many critical theorists draw particular inspiration from the work of an Italian Marxist thinker called Antonio Gramsci. Gramsci, writing in early twentieth century Italy, sought to explain why it was that the working classes continued to support the capitalist system, even though it seemed to have led to considerable impoverishment. Why was it that these working class people did not partake in revolutionary politics that might lead to the overthrow of the regime? Gramsci introduced the concept of *hegemony* to explain how the capitalist system had become accepted by all as the best economic system. Hegemony not only consists of a coercive element (how political violence by the state played a role in deterring rebellion) but also operates through consent (the way in which the values of the richest social classes come to be viewed as 'common-sense' values). Hegemony therefore is about the subtle forms of ideological control and manipulation perpetuated within what is called civil society (through things like the educational system, church and the media) that serve to shore up the repressive and exploitative structures that underpin capitalist society.

Writers like Robert Cox and Stephen Gill (often referred to as Neo-Gramscians) have sought to apply this concept of hegemony to the global level. They put forward the idea that the development of a transnational hegemony is taking place. We will look again at this idea in Chapter 7, but the basic idea is that international capital has a special status and enhanced power in today's global economy. Cox argues that the state-centric view of realism obscures the extent to which power in world politics is not confined to states but is manifested in the exercise of power by 'social forces'. The influence of an increasingly global class of capitalists on and within international institutions, states and MNCs would be an example of the idea of the power of social forces in world politics. The concept of hegemony nicely encapsulates the idea that these powerful social groupings, unconstrained by national boundaries, are able to reproduce their political dominance through a combination of coercion and consent.

In explaining how to combat this hegemonic world order, Cox again utilizes another Gramscian concept – that of counter-hegemony. To overturn a hegemonic order, there must be an alternative ideology supported by social groups from different classes. A current example of this global counter-hegemony, it has been suggested by Neo-Gramscians, might be found in the so-called 'anti-Globalization' movement (see Chapter 7) (Eschle and Maiguashca 2005). It is through the concept of counter-hegemony that the Neo-Gramscians develop an emancipatory theory of IR (one that is committed to overturning repressive hierarchies that act to confine certain groups of people to the lowest social orders). Neo-Gramscian critical theory therefore is more than simply a 'critique' of current modes of thinking about world politics – it also presents us with an alternative vision or, returning to the idea introduced at the start of this chapter, 'picture' of IR: an emancipatory theory of social change on a global scale which is rooted in an examination of the linkage between social forces, ideology, hegemony and capitalism.

POSTMODERNISM

Postmodernism (also known as post-structuralism) is in many ways the post-positivist theory par excellence. It is an approach that is based above all on the questioning of knowledge claims, and focused on exposing the linkages between knowledge creation and power. This is a concern that reflects the work of the postmodernist philosopher Foucault, who discussed the way in which power and knowledge create each other (they are mutually supportive). Thus for postmodernists like the critical theorists, knowledge and our understanding of the world are not neutral or 'common-sense' but reflect dominant power relations in society.

As an approach within IR, postmodernism is very much at the margins of the discipline. In part, this is because of the way in which it evolved outside of the social sciences in areas such as literary criticism and cultural studies. However, international relations has been especially hostile to the development of a postmodernist perspective. Critics have bemoaned the usage of the highly theoretical language of postmodern analysis and have challenged the attack on scientific standards – asking how can rigorous theories that have practical applications in the 'real world' be developed without some attachment to basic social scientific principles (Østerud 1996: 389). In response, postmodernists argue that postmodernism should not be judged by the same standards as the positivist and classical theories of IR that sought to define certain 'facts' about the world. For postmodernists the purpose of their intellectual project is *not* to come up with a testable theory of how the world works, but rather to bring critical and normative concerns into the realm of IR by exposing the power structures that produce the mainstream theoretical categories (Smith 1997).

Central to the postmodernist approach, then, is an attack on something called *metanarratives* – theories tied to a particular set of 'truth claims' about the world. Postmodernists suggest that adopting a foundational epistemology (a view of the world rooted in such truth claims) is highly problematic. This is because they suggest that there can be no objective knowledge of the world – no basis upon which we can make these claims to a universal position of 'truth'. So the supposed objectivity of a theory such as neo-realism is exposed as reflecting more the subjective biases, assumptions and identities of those scholars who put forward neo-realist theories of IR. That most neo-realist scholars were white middle class men based in North America matters to postmodernists because this positioning as members of one of the most highly privileged groups in society plays a role in shaping their view of the world and their theoretical disposition towards it.

The neo-realist perspective has been a particular target of the postmodern scholar Richard Ashley (1984, 1988). Ashley took issue with the way in which neo-realism presented a totalizing view of international politics in which everything was explained in reference to a simplistic attachment to the structural qualities of anarchy. Neo-realism thus curtailed the possibility for alternative views of international politics to emerge – effectively shutting down debate. The eschewing of foundationalist perspective and the call for debate and dialogue in IR by postmodernist scholars has often been interpreted by critics of postmodernism as a failure to come up with an alternative perspective on IR. The most commonly made criticism of postmodernism is that it exists as little more than a critique (Walt 1998). However, such positions somewhat miss the point of postmodern analysis. As Ashley points out, the point of theory is not to replace one totalizing and hegemonic view of international politics with another but to undermine such tendencies. Thus a postmodern position enables that

> practices might be resisted or disabled; boundaries might be put into doubt and transgressed; representations might be subverted, deprived of the presumption of self-evidence, and politicized and historicized: new connections among diverse cultural elements might become possible; and new ways of thinking and doing global politics might be opened up.
>
> (Ashley 1988: 254)

Of course, much of what postmodernists do is very similar to that of the critical theorists. In fact some would say that postmodernism is a form of critical theory and distinguish between a postmodern critical theory and a Marxian critical theory. The difference between the two approaches lies in the postmodernist's critique of the idea of modernity. For them, modernity consists of the belief, made popular during the Enlightenment period of the eighteenth century, in the power of value-free scientific analysis to bring about progressive change towards a predetermined goal (or *Telos*). While (Marxian) critical theorists like Cox strongly reject the idea of value-free neutral scientific inquiry, critical theory's commitment to the notion of an emancipatory theory of social change does not totally break with the Enlightenment tradition.

In seeking to expose the relationship between knowledge and power, postmodernists have adopted a range of distinct methodological tactics. One of these is the technique of textual analysis – the analysis of language or 'texts' though deconstruction. What this involves is upsetting the notion that there are any stable concepts in the study of social phenomena and challenging the tendency in western thinking to construct boundaries around what we consider to be opposites (e.g. self and other; man and woman; reason and emotion). Thus we might take a concept like 'rationality', something that is highly privileged in realist IR, which constantly talks of the state as a rational actor and contrast that with the idea of 'emotion'. Clearly rationality is a concept that is more highly valued in mainstream IR, and our 'common sense' view is that rationality is an important virtue for any diplomat or foreign policy holder to possess. However, does the privileging of rationality over emotion reflect a world order in which violence and aggression can be reasonably defended rather than seen as abhorrent and at odds with our common humanity?

At the core of postmodernist thinking is a belief that the person studying international relations cannot be separated from the object of their studies. So whereas some theories of IR (neo-realism in particular) placed emphasis on the need for the scholar to look at the world from an impartial value-free objective standpoint, postmodernists claim that the goal of value-free neutrality can never be attained. Things like the social class, race and ethnicity, gender and nationality of the author all impinge in some way on how knowledge is created. Theories that present themselves as value-free and 'scientific' do so because being described as such adds legitimacy to the work of a scholar – but postmodernists argue instead that these theories are as unscientific, subjective and full of values and opinions as any other set of theories. As we now go on to discuss, many of these important concerns about the position of the theorist/researcher are central to feminist perspectives in IR too.

FEMINISM

Feminist IR emerged in the 1980s and provided a powerful critique of the ways in which our knowledge of IR has been shaped by the experiences of men, neglecting the very different ways in which women experience world politics. In her ground-breaking feminist study of IR, *Bananas, Beaches, and Bases: Making Feminist Sense of International Relations,* Cynthia Enloe (1989) asked the question 'where are the women?' This was an important question to ask because women were so markedly absent from the sphere of inter-national politics – women are poorly represented in all of the areas that we 'traditionally' associate with IR: as heads of state, diplomats, military officials, business leaders, heads of international organiza-tions etc. What Enloe sought to do was to suggest that women are not absent from international relations – rather, they have been overlooked. Because we define IR as to do with the 'high' politics of inter-state relations, we fail to recognize the essential yet undervalued roles that women play as diplomatic wives, workers in multinational corporations, or plantation workers.

By asking 'where are the women?', Enloe challenges our under-standing of IR and points attention to the way in which the operation of global politics (and also economics) rests upon the subordina-tion of women. Likewise, Peterson and Runyan (1999) argue that theorists of IR need to apply a 'lens of gender' – in other words, consider how thinking about gender forces us to rethink the study of IR. Most theories of IR are presented as gender-neutral, in par-ticular you will not see discussions of men and women, masculinity and femininity in most mainstream IR texts. But when we apply the lens of gender we can start to rethink the way in which these theories reflect gendered assumptions. As Pettman (1996: vii) argues, 'IR is one of the most masculinist of disciplines'. Consequently:

> It is, not coincidentally, one of the most resistant to feminist scholarship. It proceeds, largely, as if women aren't in world politics. This suggests that 'the international' is literally men's business; or possibly that women and men play similar roles and are similarly affected by international relations and processes. IR has been reluctant to attend to the politics of its own knowledge-making, including its own gender politics. It has, until very recently, and still, in many places, kept feminist scholarship – and feminists – out.

> (Pettman 1996: vii)

Feminists have drawn attention to the way in which we construct certain ideas about male and female characteristics. Typically, men are viewed as strong, violent yet also rational. Women are viewed as passive, caring and emotional (feminists do not say that women and men are naturally like this but that these are socially constructed categories that shape the way in which we think about gender difference). Thinking in terms of these categories we can see that both realism and neo-realism – with their emphasis on rational states struggling to survive in a hostile and violent world – is a theory that has clearly been devised with masculinist assumptions in mind.

There are a number of different grounds on which feminists seek to challenge the validity of the realist and neo-realist perspectives. First, they criticize the overemphasis on violence, aggression and competition found in realist thought. Writers like Morgenthau based their understanding of realism on certain claims about human nature (egoistic, competitive, violent). Feminists have challenged this idea asking, who are the humans who are the model for this behaviour (Pettman 1996: 92)? For feminists, then, what Morganthau does can be labelled 'androcentricism' – taking characteristics associated with masculinity and universalizing them. The value placed on rationality and rational action in much IR theory is another example of androcentricism – privileging qualities associated with masculinity over qualities associated with femininity. Many feminists have also drawn upon postmodernist methodologies such as discourse analysis in order to deconstruct the masculinist biases that are built into the very language of IR. Carol Cohn (1987) employs textual analysis, for example, in her study of the way in which the language of international relations is grounded in masculinist assumptions. The rational, detached 'technostrategic language' (Cohn 1987: 715) of 'defence intellectuals' present defence strategies in an objective pseudo-scientific language that obscures the devastating humanitarian impact of conflict.

Second, feminists challenge the way in which the state has conventionally been understood in much IR theory. Mainstream IR simply assumes that international politics is something that is conducted by sovereign states – but, as Jill Steans (1998) points out, such a simplistic formulation can be contested on a number of grounds by applying insights from feminism. The tendency of realist IR to focus purely on relations between states obscures the extent to which things happen below the state, effectively assigning the study of gender relations to a domestic realm that has no place in the 'high politics' of the international realm. In this sense, IR scholars are able to maintain the useful fiction of gender neutrality because gender is not seen to have a legitimate place within the study of international politics. However, feminists have pointed out that understandings of the state as 'gender-neutral' obscure the extent to which states have acted to institutionalize gender inequality throughout their legal and bureaucratic structures and policy practices. Furthermore, the formation of the modern 'sovereign' state in international politics is linked to ideas of 'the nation' as an autonomous political entity (hence 'nation-states'). But as a number of scholars have pointed out, nationalism is a highly gendered ideology that emerged in the nineteenth century and contained a number of assumptions about the 'proper' role of men and women in society (Yuval-Davis and Anthias 1989). While most IR theory takes the category of the state for granted, feminist IR raises important concerns about the actual male dominance found in most states around the world and the processes whereby states have emerged as gendered – as 'manly states' (Hooper 2001). As Pettman points out, 'it is simply not possible to explain state power without explaining women's systematic exclusion from it' (Pettman 1996: 5).

Third, specific criticisms are made of those mainstream theories of IR such as neo-realism that adopt positivist methods. Like the postmodernists, many feminists suggest that explanations of IR can never be devised in a value free, objective manner. Thus the dominance of male scholars within the academic discipline of IR is manifested in the androcentric bias of the discipline. The attachment to rational objective social-scientific method found in mainstream positivist IR theory is itself indicative of the male bias within the discipline. Robert Keohane (1991, 1998), for example, argued that feminist scholarship needed to develop a clearer more 'scientific' research programme (and to eschew its association with postmodernism) – while the feminist IR scholar J. Ann Tickner (1997) responded 'You just don't understand'! The extent to which mainstream IR has misunderstood and misinterpreted the core claims of feminist IR are perhaps most successfully overviewed in an article by Steans (2003).

Finally, feminists raise concerns about the level of abstraction in IR theories such as neo-realism. Positivist approaches in IR generate a discipline that is all about objective 'scientific' values rather than the ways in which international politics touches down and impacts on the everyday lives of ordinary people. Youngs (2004) labels this feminist reformulation of international politics 'ontological revisionism' – a process whereby scholars go beyond accepted definitions (for example of the state) to show how these definitions mask and disguise gendered power relations (and other forms of social power relations). Thus one benefit of feminist IR is that it has opened up a space for the 'voices of the disadvantaged' to be brought into the discipline. While certain feminist IR scholars take what is known as a 'feminist standpoint' – looking at international politics from the perspective of women, it has increasingly come to be acknowledged that there are many feminist positions that are mediated by differences of race, ethnicity, religion, sexuality and class. Thus, some of the most interesting feminist IR scholarship to emerge in recent years draws upon developments in postcolonial theory to build a more reflective approach to feminist theorizing, one that acknowledges the unique perspectives and experiences of 'the South' in reconstructing international political agendas (Chowdhry and Nair 2002).

CONSTRUCTIVISM

A constructivist position on international politics has increasingly come to be accepted as an important theoretical position in international relations. Constructivists share the view that all knowledge of the world is 'socially constructed' – it reflects our own prejudices, ideas and assumptions rather than some kind of objective social reality. Constructivism, therefore, like other approaches overviewed in this chapter, challenges the extent to which international politics can be treated as a positivist social *science* because it looks at how things like norms, ideas and culture play a role in the construction of political realities (Williams 1998: 208). In this sense, international politics is fundamentally a reflection of people's ideas about the world rather than a reflection of material forces that shape people's experiences of the world. However, some ideas that we have about the world are much more influential than others –for example ideas such as 'the state matters in international relations' or 'globalization is changing the nature of international politics' are commonly held views. It is these commonly held views that constructivists are particularly interested in; their aim is to focus on how consensus emerges around particular ideas – how certain ideas come to have the status of 'facts' in international politics. These ideas are frequently referred to as 'inter-subjective beliefs'; they are socially constructed ideas but are widely regarded as being true.

Furthermore, inter-subjective beliefs such as these are a reflection of how socially constructed notions of an actor's identity shape their interests in international politics. Thus, for example, the belief that 'the primary role of the state is to seek security in the national interest' enables a state to construct its identity as a unitary and rational actor and its (national) interest as seeking to strengthen its military and economic power in order to ensure 'security' and survival. This argument is summarized by Alexander Wendt when he makes the claim that 'identities are the basis of interests' (Wendt 1992: 397). However, identities are themselves the product of inter-subjective beliefs; they are not fixed, rather they are relational (defined in relation to the identities and interests of other actors). One of the most important implications of this social constructivist turn has been to focus on the relationship between the ideational (i.e. socially constructed inter-subjective beliefs) and the material (the 'real world' of security and economics in which international political activity takes place). It is on this issue that we can see a distinction between constructivism and other traditions of IR scholarship.

First, constructivism differs from those positivist approaches to IR such as neo-realism that emphasize the material role of international anarchy in structuring actor (i.e. state) behaviour. Constructivists stress the way in which those structures that shape actor behaviour are the product of inter-subjective beliefs (Wendt 1994: 385). So when Alexander Wendt (1992) argued 'Anarchy is what states make of it', what he was suggesting was that the idea of anarchy in international politics is just that – an idea – but a powerful and influential idea that all states have bought into and believe to exist. Wendt shares the view that neo-realists hold that international politics operates under conditions of anarchy and that anarchy has a structural quality, but suggests that the reason why this anarchical system exists has more to do with how states come to define their interests and identities (as sovereign states).

Wendt isn't so much challenging the structuralism of neo-realism as its very conception of structure. Neo-realists see structure as fixed and unchanging – anarchy to them is a basic condition of international politics that acts to regulate and constrain how actors behave. Neo-realism is what we might call a structurally deterministic theory – the structure explains everything. This is seen as a problem by Wendt because there is no explanation granted as to why these structures exist in the first place. Furthermore, there is no possibility for change within such a structurally deterministic view of the world. Constructivist understandings of international politics do open up some possibility for change because if anarchy exists on the basis of inter-subjective beliefs rooted in human activity then they can be (slowly) transcended. Constructivism, therefore, seeks to break down the sharp demarcation between structure and agency (as understood in terms of the relationship between sovereign states (agents) and international anarchy) that characterizes much IR thinking.

But by accepting that anarchy has a structural quality – albeit one that is inter-subjective rather than material, critics suggest that Wendt endorses an approach that looks to the construction of state identity purely in terms of the state's relationships with other states in the system and critics argue that he fails to consider how state identity formation also reflects domestic processes (Zehfuss 2002). This is not, however, typical of all constructivist scholarship. Peter Katzenstein, for example, has throughout his work sought to explore the relationship between domestic interests and international interests and the role that ideas play in shaping political outcomes. For example in the article 'Why is There no NATO in Asia', Hemmer and Katzenstein (2002) explore how US policy towards Asia during the Cold War was mediated by quite racist ideas about Asia deeply rooted in American political culture and notions of the USA's identity as a 'Western' nation. (These constructions of Asia were, in turn, met by reconstructions of an Asian regional identity within Asia – a discussion that we considered in more depth in Chapter 5 Box 5.2).

Second, we should draw attention to the way in which constructivism differs from postmodernism. Both perspectives stress the importance of social-construction; however, for the postmodernist, the appeal of social construction lies in the way that a recognition of the socially constructed nature of the world can enable us to challenge our core beliefs, values and ways of knowing – challenging the very notion that a 'real world' exists. In this sense, postmodernism is an anti-foundationalist position. By contrast, most constructivist scholars seek to accept that there is some kind of objective social reality, but that processes of social construction have played a role in its emergence. Perhaps, then, one of the best ways of thinking about the constructivists in IR is that they are seeking to develop some kind of 'third way' between a positivist and post-positivist approach (Adler 1997; Checkel 1997).

However, much constructivist scholarship specifically seeks to engage with more 'rationalist' approaches to the discipline, than with the other post-positivist approaches discussed in this chapter. Indeed, many would challenge whether constructivist scholarship is post-positivist at all given that many constructivist scholars have merely sought to add on a concern with ideas and identities into their 'problem solving' and highly depoliticized approach to theorizing (Sterling-Folker 2000; Teschke and Heine 2002). Furthermore, certain constructivist concerns about the role of ideas, norms and culture have been straightforwardly 'added on' to the work of traditionally positivist scholars – seeing it as a means by which to mop up 'other variables' in their work (see for example Goldstein and Keohane 1993).

But adopting constructivist understandings concerning the relationship between the ideational and the material is not in itself an act of depoliticization. Reus-Smit (2005) argues that constructivist thinkers need to move away from their tendency to engage with rationalist IR and instead to adopt a concern with normative and ethical issues that would move constructivism away from a 'problem solving' approach to theory and towards something that can enable a more emancipatory approach to international political theorizing. For example, Locher and Prügl (2001) have argued for constructivists to take more seriously some of the important political questions about how knowledge is produced raised by feminist IR. This engagement might be one route through which a more politicized, emancipatory and ultimately more post-positivist constructivism could be developed. We discuss further some of these more critical social constructivist approaches in the discussion of globalization found in Chapter 8.

WHAT POST-POSITIVISM MEANT/MEANS FOR THE STUDY OF IR

You may have noticed that the post-positivist traditions in IR emerged during the late 1980s and early 1990s. What was the significance of this date? Why was it that it was only then that the discipline was ripe for such a fundamental challenge to its methodological foundations? After all, feminism as a political doctrine had been around since the eighteenth century, postmodernism had its roots in the 1940s and critical theory owes a heavy debt to the work of both nineteenth and early twentieth century Marxism. Why was it that all three of these intellectual traditions had been ignored for so long by IR?

The answer lies partially in the historical circumstances of the late 1980s. The end of the Cold War opened up a space for challenging the way in which we think about international relations. Realism and neo-realism in particular offered such a convenient explanation of the Cold War, yet failed to predict the end of this conflict (after all, neo-realism is an ahistorical theory – it allows no room for change). Naturally, into this theoretical void stepped many idealist and English school thinkers (Kegley 1993), but it also created a space for a rethink of the very foundations of the subject.

All three of the post-positivist theories that we have looked at reflect a certain shift within IR towards thinking that is normative and critical (and to a certain extent – especially in the case of feminism and critical theory – emancipatory). The ethical turn in IR is an issue that we develop at greater depth in later chapters of this book. What this chapter has served to highlight is that the space for studies of IR that seek simply to describe their version of reality is becoming increasingly challenged.

TOPICS FOR DISCUSSION

1 Do you agree or disagree with the view that the study of IR can be treated as a science?
2 Is there a coherent post-positivist position in IR? What concerns do most post-positivist scholars share?
3 What did Robert Cox mean when he argued 'theory is always for someone and some purpose'?
4 What does it mean to apply the 'lens of gender'?
5 How can we 'deconstruct' neo-realist IR theory?
6 Are you convinced by Alexander Wendt's argument that 'anarchy is what states make of it'?

FURTHER READING

GENERAL: THEORIES AND THEORISTS

Burchill, S. and Linklater, A. *et al.* (eds) (2005) *Theories of International Relations*, third edition, Basingstoke: Palgrave MacMillan.

Griffiths, M. (1999) *Fifty Key Thinkers in International Relations*. London: Routledge. See entries on Robert Cox, Alexander Wendt, Richard Ashley, Cynthia Enloe and J. Ann Tickner.

Brown, C. with Ainley, K. (2005) *Understanding International Relations*, third edition. Basingstoke: Palgrave Macmillan. See Chapter 3.

Smith, S. and Owens, P. (2005) 'Alternative Approaches to International Theory', in J. Baylis and S. Smith (eds) *The Globalization of World Politics: An Introduction to International Relations*, third Edition, Oxford: Oxford University Press, pp. 271–290.

METHODOLOGICAL DEBATES

Jackson, R. and Sørenson, G. (2003) *Introduction to International Relations: Theories and Approaches*, second edition, Oxford: Oxford University Press. See Chapters 8 and 9.

Lapid, Y. (1989) 'The Third Debate: On the Prospects of International Theory in a Post-Positivist Era', *International Studies Quarterly* 33: 235–254.

Smith, S., Booth, K. and Zalewski, M. (eds) (1996) *International Theory: Positivism and Beyond, Cambridge:* Cambridge University Press.

CRITICAL THEORY

Cox, R.W. (1996) *Approaches to World Order*, Cambridge: Cambridge University Press.

POSTMODERNISM

Ashley, R. (1988) 'Untying the Sovereign State: a Double Reading of the Anarchy Problematique', *Millennium: Journal of International Studies* 17 (2): 227–262.

GENDER

Steans, J. (1998) *Gender and International Relations: An Introduction*, Cambridge: Polity Press.

CONSTRUCTIVISM

Wendt, A. (1992) 'Anarchy is What States Make of It: the Social Construction of Power Politics', *International Organization*, 46 (2): 391–426.

7

RECONFIGURING WORLD POLITICS

Globalization

Students taking a course in international politics might reasonably expect their studies to touch on issues relating to war and peace in the international system, diplomacy, foreign policy making, and international organizations such as the United Nations. Students might be less inclined to think that international politics is about international trade, money and finance, economic policy making, migration or global poverty and inequality. Indeed, within the academic study of international relations, it has generally been the case that economic issues have been viewed as of lesser important to the 'high politics' of inter-state relations. In this chapter, we challenge this realist perspective through a discussion of one of the major subfields of IR – international political economy (IPE) – and introducing you to the concept of globalization which has been a major focus of IPE scholarship.

Introducing globalization however is no easy task – Rosenberg (2000: 11) has pointed out, for example, that 'we live today in a veritable "age of globalization studies"' – and we certainly have no intention of taking you through *all* of the literature on globalization in one short chapter! Furthermore, we do not aim to provide you with a comprehensive definition of what globalization is, but rather to introduce you to the (hotly contested) debates surrounding the

issue of globalization. Most importantly, we raise questions concerning the relationship between globalization and the state. This is
an issue of central importance to the study of IR, not least because
if we are forced to rethink the way in which states behave, then we
also have to rethink the validity of the realist paradigm that you
were introduced to in earlier chapters of the book.

BRINGING IN AN INTERNATIONAL POLITICAL ECONOMY PERSPECTIVE

A recognition of the intertwined nature of politics and economics
gave rise, in the 1970s, to a new approach in IR known as international
political economy. IPE has its roots in what in the eighteenth and
nineteenth centuries was called 'political economy' – essentially the
study of economic activity within political and legal contexts. The
best known political economists include Adam Smith, author of the
eighteenth century liberal treatise on political economy *The Wealth
of Nations*, and Karl Marx, the radical nineteenth century philosopher and revolutionary. In the twentieth century, political economy
was carved up into the separate disciplines of political science and
economics, so in a sense, IPE represents a return to a more holistic
approach to understanding the social world – albeit one in which
understanding the relationship between politics and economics
requires that we place such an analysis within an *international* (or
perhaps more appropriately a *global*) context.

While scholars such as Jacob Viner writing in the 1940s paid
attention to the study of 'power and wealth' in international politics
(Viner 1948), it is the British academic, Susan Strange, who is often
credited with the promotion of IPE as a key area of international
studies (Brown 1999). Clearly echoing the roots of the discipline
within political economy, Strange presented the discipline as
concerning the study of the relationship between 'the state and the
market' (Strange 1994a). Many early scholars of IPE tended to
emphasize how economic bargaining between states was just as
important a form of diplomacy as bargaining between states over
issues such as territorial possessions or peace agreements (Spero
1990). Some writers within IPE still basically adhere to the view that
economic diplomacy is just one of the many tools that states utilize

to ensure their relative gains *vis-à-vis* other states. So things like economic sanctions, bargaining over trade at the World Trade Organization, creating agreements over illegal immigration or deciding to join a single European currency are all decisions that states take in their own national interest with an eye on how such agreements might impact on the power status of other states. In this more 'realist' view of IPE, states remain the central and most important actors using economic tools such as tariffs and economic sanctions to secure the most power.

However, most IPE scholars do not adhere to this realist (or 'economic nationalist') perspective. In fact, early writings in an IPE tradition have tended to emphasize the limitations of thinking about inter-state relations solely in terms of power relations. Authors such as Keohane and Nye (1977), for example (the neo-liberal institutionalists that we came across in earlier chapters) were keen to stress the role of international economic interdependency in building and supporting what they called 'complex interdependency'. In this liberal view, the growing levels of interdependence in the international economy are more important than states' desires to constantly outdo each other. A liberal IPE tradition has therefore placed emphasis on the way in which growing levels of economic interdependency and the spread of free trade has undermined the self-interested (i.e. realist) behaviours of states; in this view then, the economic sphere is always going to be much more important than the political imperatives of states. The emphasis on economic interdependency found in these writings has been expanded and developed in recent years as IPE scholars began to incorporate analysis of a phenomenon known as globalization into their studies of the international system.

What should become clear from this chapter is that while liberalism is one of the dominant IPE perspectives in analyses of globalization, it is only one of many perspectives on globalization. Remember back to Chapter 1 in which we argued that realism was the dominant perspective in IR and that this perspective has been challenged by a number of alternative, and critical perspectives. Well within IPE, realism has taken much more of a back seat – here it is liberalism that has come to be recognised as the 'mainstream' of IPE scholarship. On the one hand, we can point to an overtly positivist liberal political economy that draws upon liberal economic theory, presenting understandings of globalization that view it largely as an inevitable economic process. Often this scholarship can be associated with a neo-liberal turn in economic theory – the view that the state should not play a significant role in the economy and that policies of privatization and deregulation are the best means through which economies can remain competitive. Importantly, when we discuss neo-liberalism in the context of this chapter we are discussing neo-liberalism as an economic theory (indeed perhaps *the* most influential economic theory). Make sure that you keep this point in mind because often within IR the term neo-liberalism is employed when referring to the work of neo-liberal institutionalists (such as Keohane and Nye). On the other hand, we can identify liberal thinkers who take a less economically neo-liberal line – arguing that global capitalism, if properly regulated, can bring about positive social change and prosperity for all (Cerny 2000; Giddens 2000). However, it is the economically neo-liberal understanding of political economy that is by far the most influential of the two; it has influenced the economic policies of states around the world and is widely regarded as the economic philosophy that underpins powerful international financial institutions such as the IMF and the World Bank.

Outside of the liberal mainstream we can identify some important alternative perspectives. Most notable of these alternative perspectives is the work of scholars associated with Marxist political economy. Indeed, Robert Gilpin (1987) has argued that alongside liberalism and economic nationalism (realism), Marxism is one of the major ideologies of political economy. That being said, it has also been argued that Marxist perspectives in IPE have remained largely at the margins – and that Marxist and Marxian approaches are especially marginalized when one looks at the discipline of IR as a whole (Bieler and Morton 2003).

There are a wide range of competing Marxist and Marxian understandings of globalization. If you pursue an interest in IPE during your course of studies you will no doubt come across some of these different Marxian literatures; most notably you are likely to come across the work of Robert Cox and a group of Marxist inspired scholars called the neo-Gramscians. What these perspectives have in common is that they share a concern with the way in which relations of class domination (and therefore inequality) are a fundamental feature of the expansion of capitalist production that is taking place in an era of globalization. In this view, therefore, globalization *is* capitalism and the analytical tools and ideas that Marx developed in the nineteenth century in relation to the study of the development of a capitalist mode of production are just as relevant for analysing globalizing capitalism today. Take this quotation from the *Communist Manifesto*, which was first published in 1848 for example:

> The bourgeoisie has through its exploitation of the world market given a cosmopolitan character to production and consumption in every country. . . . All old-fashioned national industries have been destroyed or are daily being destroyed. . . . In place of the old local and national seclusion and self-sufficiency, we have intercourse in every direction, universal independence of nations.
>
> (Marx and Engels 1992: 6)

The above quotation shows clearly that Marx (and his collaborator Friedrich Engels) observed, even back in the nineteenth century, the way in which capitalism was taking on a global character. However, this is not a straightforward analysis of the emergence of a global market economy akin to that put forward by many economic liberals. The emphasis on 'exploitation' of workers by a dominant capitalist class (the 'bourgeoisie') identifies Marxism as a critical approach to the study of globalization – one in which normative concerns about the oppression of marginalized peoples are central to developing a critique of globalization as capitalism. We find similar concerns about exploitation and marginalization in the feminist literature on globalization where the claim is made that the emergence of a global economy has entrenched systems of inequality – particularly gender inequality – creating a feminization of global poverty (Joekes 1987; Razavi 1999; Rai 2002). How these criticisms of globalization have resulted in attempts to develop alternative, emancipatory, perspectives on globalization is a theme that we develop in the final section of this chapter where we look at resistances to globalization.

UNDERSTANDING GLOBALIZATION

One of the most commonly used definitions of globalization is David Harvey's expression 'time space compression' (Harvey 1989). This relates to the idea that we are now living in a 'global village', all increasingly interconnected and closer to one another. Harvey's idea of 'time space compression' expresses the idea that time is increasingly eradicating space – that the time that it takes for people and goods to move around the planet today has been significantly diminished by developments in things like communication technologies and transportation. The phrase 'globalization' has become common parlance in the media and politics since the 1980s and yet, what is lacking is any real agreement as to what globalization actually is. As Brenner (1999: 3) has pointed out, globalization is what might be termed an 'essentially contested concept'. This means that there is no agreement whatsoever as to what globalization is, whether it is even happening and, more fundamentally how we ascribe meaning (understand, interpret, analyse) the processes associated with globalization. Furthermore, debates also rage about the impact of globalization in terms of the widening of inequality and the globalization of poverty.

Many liberal scholars would argue that globalization is opening up opportunities for some of the poorest countries and people in the world. For example, the opening of a large call centre industry in a country such as India has been the result of processes that we generally associate with globalization such as the growth in foreign direct investment by MNCs and the rapid global spread of communication technologies. An economic liberal analyst would point to the positive outcomes of these investments, showing how they provide new opportunities for employment, which in turn has beneficial effects on the whole local economy. However, critics would point to the widening social inequalities that often accompany these types of investments, so call centres may provide much needed employment in countries like India, but it is only the relatively wealthy and well educated who are able to take advantage of these new opportunities. For the vast majority of a country's rural poor, poverty is as much a feature of their daily existence as it ever was.

MULTIDIMENSIONAL GLOBALIZATION

Standard definitions of globalization associate it with a number of different processes of change – the idea that something has fundamentally altered in the world that we live in today. In this chapter, we focus on three different 'dimensions' of globalization – the economic, the cultural and the political. However, this is not to suggest that we are putting forward a coherent definition of what globalization IS. Rather our aim here is to overview many of the different processes that have come to be included with definitions of globalization. It should be noted at this point, however, that separating out the economic, political and cultural dimensions of globalization is a somewhat artificial process – in fact, we would suggest all three of these processes are, in different ways, inextricably bound-up with one another.

AN ECONOMIC DIMENSION

Discussions of globalization often focus on a definition of globalization that views it almost entirely as an economic phenomenon. The changing nature of production (how goods are manufactured) is one of the most obvious dimensions of economic globalization (Dicken, 2003). The production of goods in today's global economy looks very different compared to the early twentieth century when industrial production was dominated by a few states in North America, Europe and, in Asia, Japan. The growth of faster transportation and communications links has meant that many firms have sought to relocate some of the more labour-intensive elements of their production process to countries where labour costs are significantly cheaper. The production of manufactured goods has also become increasingly complex – in the production of clothing for example, there are vast networks of small firms that produce clothing for the major brands like The Gap or Levis. Often these brands have no real idea where their products are being made at all. Service sector industries have also become increasingly global. We now have global media empires, call centres located in Bangalore servicing the European and American market, and huge global management consultancy, insurance and banking corporations.

An important element of the processes associated with economic globalization is the growth of what we might term a global financial market (that revolves around the trading of different currencies and other financial products against one another). Large investment banks have grown in power and influence on the back of their ability to make massive profits from currency fluctuations (the constantly changing value of currencies). New technologies not only have increased the speed at which we can travel and communicate, but also have made possible the electronic transfer of money, so that money can move across the world at the press of a button. The easy transfer of money across state boundaries is no doubt something that you will have experienced if you have travelled abroad and have used your ATM card to withdraw cash. So obviously, the electronic transfer of money is in some respects a good thing because it is a convenient technology that has contributed to making our lives easier. However, the easy flow of money across state boundaries can also have quite devastating consequences in times of financial crisis. Such is the significance of global financial markets today that a currency collapse in one part of the world can affect other states around the world in rapid succession. In July 1997, the collapse of the currency in Thailand triggered currency and stock market collapses in Indonesia, Malaysia, the Philippines and South Korea as investors rushed to pull out from these states. These events are now referred to as the Asian Financial Crisis. The crisis sent shock waves around the world and is widely viewed as a significant turning point in the economic and political history of these Asian nations. What the Asian Financial Crisis example shows is that economic events in one country can have significant knock-on effects elsewhere, and this is more the case than ever before. For many, this level of economic interdependence is evidence that we now live in a globalized world economy.

Importantly though one issue that is often swept aside in discussions of economic globalization is the role of labour. In part, there is a good reason for this – whereas capital finds it increasingly easy to roam around the world – this has not been the case for workers (Munck 2002; Castree et al. 2004). Witness the massive debates concerning immigration and asylum that have taken place in almost all states in the industrialized world in recent years. Indeed, there has been a progressive tightening of borders – it was far easier to move round the world in the nineteenth century than it is today. However, a number of studies have sought to examine how globalization impacts upon workers employed in some of the world's most globalized industries – garment manufacture, electronic goods assembly, call centre employment and tourism (Freeman 2000; Rosen 2002; Salzinger 2003; Adler and Adler 2004; Elias 2004). What these studies point to is the great efficiency with which global corporations are able to source supplies of low cost labour from around the world. In this context, states are often portrayed as competing to attract foreign direct investment through things like restrictions on trade union activities or lowering of minimum wages. Importantly, this is a process that has taken place in *both* developed and developing countries.

A CULTURAL DIMENSION

Understandings of globalization have extended beyond these economic processes and have sought also to look at the cultural dimensions of globalization (Stevenson 2000). Some would suggest, for example, that the peoples of the world are becoming more similar in terms of their tastes, values and expectations; that businesses are increasingly pursuing the same kinds of practices; and we are increasingly watching the same TV shows, eating the same foods, shopping in the same shops.

Some would argue that cultural globalization is a process whereby all peoples of the world are becoming culturally similar or, at the very least, are being exposed to the same cultural values and products. One view of cultural globalization, therefore, equates it with a process of universalization whereby we are all becoming culturally more and more alike. For others, this is not universalization, but Westernization – witness the increasingly widespread use of the English language for example. Ideas of universalization and Westernization appear in the work of the liberal scholar Francis Fukuyama. Fukuyama famously argued that we had reached an 'end of history' with the ending of the Cold War and that all peoples of the world had embraced 'universal' values of democracy, human rights and, importantly, a capitalist economic system – values that have their roots in the economic, cultural and political systems of the West (Fukuyama

1992). In this liberal-informed perspective on globalization, an emerging cultural homogeneity is viewed as a positive development and, indeed, a force for peace and prosperity.

Others, while accepting that processes of cultural globalization are taking place, seek to challenge the extent to which this is a positive development. It has been suggested, for example, that diverse national cultures are being swept away in favour of a new global culture based almost entirely on the consumption of standardized products like Big Mac hamburgers or Nike training shoes. This point of view sees the hand of big business corporations in undermining cultural diversity in order to sell as many consumer products to us as possible. Hence cultural globalization has also been labelled 'McDonaldization' – whereby individuals emerge simply as consumers of mass produced goods. The hallmark of this global culture for writers such as Leslie Sklair (2002) is a worldwide commitment to a culture of consumerism that works in the interests of big business. Others have introduced the idea that cultural globalization is effectively a process of 'Americanization', a process whereby the cultural hegemony (that is to say, dominance) of the United States acts to back up its political and economic hegemony. Gender theorists of globalization also employ ideas of cultural hegemony. R.W. Connell (2005), for example, has suggested that the emergence of a global capitalist economic system is rooted in a particular form of gender politics whereby cultural values and attributes associated with a Western, male, middle class business elite are privileged. This 'hegemonic masculinity' underpins the dominant status of a certain class of (business) men in contemporary global politics.

A POLITICAL DIMENSION

When thinking about globalization as a political process, it is important to recognise that what we are *not* talking about is the emergence of a new supranational form of global government. But what has increasingly crept into the language of IR, as we saw in Chapter 4, are discussions of 'global governance' which might be understood as frameworks of rules set up to tackle global problems that have been agreed upon by both international organizations and national governments. Thus for example, we have seen an emerging consensus around how to deal with issues like international trade, environmental degradation and human rights.

Discussions of global governance have been criticized by many. The argument has been put forward, for example, that the concept focuses on technical fixes to current global problems but fails to investigate how emerging systems of global governance may in fact reflect the interests of the most powerful/privileged states and/or groups of people in the world today (Cammack 2002; Overbeek 2005). Thus for example, should the World Trade Organization be regarded as an institution offering all countries of the world practical help in adjusting their economies to free trade? Or should it be viewed as an institution that legitimizes an economic system based on free trade and neo-liberalism that works to the advantage of richer countries?

But talk of global governance is not the only thing to consider when looking at the political dimension to globalization. More generally, ideas have been raised about the 'reconfiguration' of political power that many have come to define as integral to understandings of globalization (Held and McGrew 2002: 9–24). One element of this reconfiguration are the debates that rage over the role of the state in an era of globalization (a debate that we focus on in more detail below). But ideas of globalization as a political process involve a number of other complex issues. For example, recent years have seen a fragmentation of political power as the end of the Cold War brought about a multitude of 'new' states in East and Central Europe and the former Soviet Union. The years since the Cold War have also witnessed a rising tide of nationalist politics, separatist movement in places like Chechnya, East Timor and Kurdistan and a devolution of national government in places such as the British Isles. On top of these developments, as we saw in Chapter 5, there has also been a consolidation of political power into regional alliances and regional organizations such as the European Union and ASEAN. Although we are commonly presented with a picture of globalization that shows states losing power to global forces, globalization also appears to unleash oppositional, contradictory forces. The years of 'globalization', therefore, have ironically also been the years of rising nationalism. Some would suggest that these two processes go hand in hand, that fragmentation is the inevitable corollary of globalization, as national cultures look inwards to protect themselves from the perceived threat of globalization. As Anthony Giddens (2000) argues:

> Most people think of globalisation as simply 'pulling away' power or influence from local communities and nations into the global arena. And indeed this is one of its consequences. Nations do lose some of the economic power they once had. Yet it also has the opposite effect. Globalisation not only pulls upwards, but also pushes downwards, creating new pressures for local autonomy.
>
> (Giddens 2000: 31)

Thus questions of governance, of where political power and authority lies, of the role of the state in international politics today are central in understanding globalization as a political process. We suggested above that the term 'global governance' can be somewhat problematic – because it often rests on assumptions that the ceding of political power to multilateral institutions and regimes is a 'good' thing. But this is not to suggest that we should abandon thinking about governance issues in the world today. As Jan Aart Scholte argues:

> The dispersal of governance in contemporary history has occurred not only across different layers and scales of social relations from the local to the global, but also alongside the emergence of various regulatory mechanisms in private quarters alongside those in the public sector. Many rules for global companies, global finance, global communications, global ecology and other global matters have been designed and administered through nongovernmental arrangements. . . . This situation of multi-scalar and diffuse governance might be called 'polycentrism', to denote its distinctive feature of emanating from multiple interconnected sites.
>
> (Scholte 2005: 86–87)

UNDERSTANDING GLOBALIZATION WITHIN IPE

As noted already in this chapter, part of this reconfiguration of political power involves questions concerning the role of the state in contemporary global politics. IPE scholarship on globalization has concentrated almost exclusively on issues concerning the reshaping or (as some would argue) the 'reimagining' of the state. In what follows, we overview the diverse IPE literatures on globalization and the state. Yet, providing an overview of a huge and diverse IPE globalization literature is no easy task. To help navigate our way through this complex literature we will apply what is called a typology – a system of classification. Borrowing from the work of Hay and Marsh (2000) we suggest that the literature on globalization in IPE is best understood in terms of a succession of 'waves' of scholarship. In some ways this 'waves' typology is rather crude; after all you will notice that not all scholars fit neatly into each category. However, typologies are a useful device to employ in order to help you to find your way through this complex topic (using typologies in this manner is often described as using a system of classification as a heuristic device).

THE FIRST WAVE: GLOBALIZATION AS THE INEVITABLE FUTURE

The first wave of globalization scholarship presents the argument that globalization is an irresistible, even inevitable, force – fundamentally reshaping global political and economic relationships. We would suggest that there are two types of first wave scholarship. One perspective has been labelled 'hyperglobalization' (Higgott and Reich 1998; Held *et al.* 1999) and 'business-globalization' (Hay and Marsh 2000; Cameron and Palan 2004). This is an extreme globalization thesis – one in which globalization is heralding the end of the nation-state as we know it. Writers such as Ohmae (1999) have argued that globalization is bringing about a 'borderless-world'. Such is the level of activity that now takes place at a global level, the state has become anachronistic, an institution that has become undermined to the point that it is no longer a useful actor in world politics. This view rests upon an extreme deterritorialization and denationalization thesis – that it is no longer possible to think about politics as taking place within territorially defined national boundaries (or 'nation-states').

Multinational corporations, presented as a driving force behind economic globalization, are placed in a centrally important role in this wave of globalization literature (hence the term 'business globalization') (Reich 1992; Barnet and Cavanagh 1996). Furthermore, this hyperglobalist/business globalization strand takes an overtly liberal approach to political economy. This means that these writers view the emergence of a global market economy and the decline in the power of the state as both a good thing and as an inevitable thing; in this sense theirs is a teleological approach to globalization attached to the ideas of progress and modernization.

Many have argued that this hyperglobalization thesis should not be taken seriously (Bruff 2005). It is regarded as too simplistic a view and one that doesn't square with what we see around us – the way in which states and territorial boundaries remain central of the everyday practice of international politics. Cameron and Palan (2004) have argued, however, that what might be termed as 'business globalization' literature is important not because it paints an accurate picture of international politics, but because it represents a highly influential set of ideas. You may well, for example, have come across the term globalization being used in the same way that Ohmae (1999) and others have employed the term. The influence of these ideas of globalization is a theme that we return to when we turn to discuss the 'third wave' of globalization scholarship.

A MODIFIED 'FIRST WAVE': GLOBALIZATION AS TRANSFORMATION

While severe doubts have been raised about the hyperglobalization school of thought, we can also identify a modified first wave of scholarship. This version presents globalization as a process that is fundamentally changing the nature of international politics – but recognises that states are able to adapt and survive in this competitive new global order. The changing nature of the state under conditions of globalization is encapsulated in Philip Cerny's (1990) concept of the 'competition state'. While the immediate post-Second World War era saw the establishment (at least in the richer, industrialized nations of the world) of welfare states committed to full employment, redistributive taxation and welfare services, today (competition) states are motivated more by the need to attract foreign investment within the context of 'the competitive rat race of the open world economy' (Cerny 1990: 229). Thus they tend to pursue neo-liberal policies such as spending cut-backs, labour market deregulation (for example getting rid of many trade union rights) and decreasing rates of taxation (especially for business).

This modified first wave of scholarship has been labelled a 'transformationalist' perspective (Higgott and Reich 1998) – the emphasis being on the 'transformation' rather than the 'end' of the state. The emergence of this literature in the late 1980s and the early 1990s offered a direct challenge to traditional (realist) IR theory. For example, scholars like Susan Strange (1994b) argued that the discipline of IR was very much out of synch with the kinds of issues that IPE scholars were concerned with. In an article entitled 'Wake Up, Krasner, the World has Changed!', Strange (1994b) berated a fellow academic for failing to take seriously the way in which globalization was changing the face of the discipline. For Strange, the realist underpinnings of IR meant that scholars like Stephen Krasner continued to write about IR as if the world was exactly the same as it had been during the Cold War – dominated by the politics of powerful states. In Strange's view such a position was untenable in a world characterized by systems of international trade, communication, money markets and production.

The transformationalist scholarship should be taken seriously because it represents a far more nuanced understanding of the relationship between globalization and the state than that provided by the hyperglobalizers. Importantly, while the transformationalist scholarship tends to view state power as being fundamentally constrained and refashioned by globalization, it also recognises that globalization is not a straightforward process of economic integration. Unlike the extreme liberal hyperglobalization position in which economic globalization is viewed as the inevitable outcome of market integration, transformationalists point to the role that states themselves played in the creation of the processes associated with globalization. In this sense states themselves enabled globalization to happen through their commitment to economic neo-liberal policies of privatization and deregulation that *enabled* money, goods and services to move quickly and easily across national boundaries. For example, the growth of global financial markets noted above was possible only because the leading economic powers agreed to deregulate their currencies in the 1970s, to move from a system of *fixed* to *floating* exchange rates (so whereas in the past currency rates did not vary considerably because states decided that they should be backed by the price of gold, today, currency prices vary according to market demand). Put simply, the transformationalist thesis is that states make globalization and globalization makes the (competition) state.

THE SECOND WAVE: GLOBAL SCEPTICISM

The second wave of IPE scholarship is, in certain respects, a reaction against the first wave. Hirst and Thompson (1999) argue in their book *Globalisation in Question* that while there is an increased level of interconnectedness in world politics today, the idea that we are entering a new era of 'globalization' is nothing more than a 'myth'. Interconnectedness (through trade, transportation etc.) has been steadily increasing throughout the centuries. Hirst and Thompson's basic thesis is that not only is there nothing 'new' about globalization, but also there is nothing 'global' about globalization. The highest levels of interconnectedness are between the most developed states in North America, Europe and East Asia, while the poorest areas of the world remain marginal to this. Take foreign direct investment as an example (when multinational firms decide to establish factories in a foreign location), very little of this goes into states in the developing world at all, it is concentrated in the 'triad' of industrialized states (North America, East Asia and Europe). In fact, the foreign investment that does go to states in the developing world tends to be concentrated in a few states such as Mexico, Brazil and China – states in Africa receive hardly any foreign investment whatsoever, further marginalizing some of the poorest countries in the world from the global economy.

Other scholars who fall within the 'sceptic' camp have pointed to the enduring capacity of states to govern their own economies (Weiss 1998). For example, states in East Asia, at least prior to the Asian crisis, have often been portrayed as states that have been able to survive and prosper in the global economy through strong state intervention in promoting export-led industrialization.

Hirst and Thompson (1999) raise another important issue – an issue that, as we shall see, has become central to the third wave of globalization scholarship, that globalization is a 'necessary myth' that states in the developed world have utilized to protect their own interests. For example, we now live in an era of global financial markets, currencies can move freely across international boundaries and large investment banks have grown wealthy on the profits to be made in the big money markets. The problem is that these global financial markets are inherently unstable: during the 1990s there were massive financial crises in Russia, Brazil and East Asia. Hirst and Thompson (1999) suggest that the major economic powers have the capacity to regulate these financial markets, but they lack the will, presenting currency collapses as an inevitable feature of the globalizing world in which we now live.

A THIRD WAVE: AN IDEATIONAL TURN

The third wave of globalization scholarship has brought together a concern with the relationship between globalization and the state with a strongly social constructivist understanding of the role of ideas in international politics. In this sense, this third wave is a critical perspective that draws upon ideas associated with the post-positivist turn in IR (see Chapter 5). At the heart of this approach lies a concern to identify globalization as a powerful discourse that plays a role in constructing the world in which we live. What this third wave scholarship forces us to do therefore is to recognise the relationship between theories of globalization and how globalization is manifested as a set of practices. As Weldes (2001) points out, we need to analyse globalization as a discourse:

> Such an approach allows us to ask what exactly a globalization discourse does. This is important because discourses are deeply political, producing significant material and ideational effects; put simply, the representations that most people entertain about globalisation – what they think globalisation is and how it works – affect how they act. It is this effect that can render globalisation discourse a self-fulfilling prophecy.
>
> (Weldes 2001: 648)

One of the concerns of the third wave is to challenge the way in which globalization regarded as a truth, a 'fact of life', or, more importantly as an inevitable process that is almost beyond human control. It is the first wave scholarship that can be criticized in this regard because these writers 'seem to accept the basic assertion that contemporary capitalism has entered a new phase' (Amoore *et al.* 1997: 179). This 'framing' of the idea of globalization is a worrying one because it presents globalization as a new phase in international politics in which nation-states are increasingly unable to deal with the attack on their sovereignty posed by this thing called globalization. Third wave scholarship therefore raises concerns about the extent to which a hyperglobalization or business globalization vision dominates our everyday understandings of contemporary processes of change in global politics. As Cameron and Palan (2004) argue:

> There is something odd at the heart of the globalization debate. The simplified version of 'business globalization', which presents globalization as a homogenous global force undermining state and society, has been far more influential than perhaps it merits on grounds of empirical rigour or theoretical sophistication.
>
> (Cameron and Palan 2004: 89)

It is this reading of the idea of globalization that creates the sense of 'no alternative' to globalization. Hay (1999, 2004) for example has criticized the way in which the Labour government in the UK have presented globalization as a force that has compelled the Labour government to abandon its socialist principles in favour of a more neo-liberal style of economic and social policy-making. As Rosamond (2003) argues:

> Of crucial importance here is the extent to which common place policy conceptions of globalization are themselves constitutive of reality; the extent to which they have so-called 'truth effects'. Thus if governments act in ways that are consistent with the tenets of the 'hyperglobalization' hypothesis, then the net effect of those actions may be the creation of a world that operates precisely in that way.
>
> (Rosamond, 2003: 666)

So what we see in this third wave is that rather than rejecting the business globalization literature outright, what is of interest is the way in which this version of globalization has shaped a social reality. For example, in the work of Cameron and Palan (2004) we are presented with the idea that a set of powerful socio-economic and political discourses (labelled 'imagined economies') have fashioned the world in which we live. These 'imagined economies' include the offshore world – a kind of hyperglobalized zone of the global economy in which MNCs roam the globe looking for cheap labour, global finance shifts around the global money markets at the push of a button and internet technologies enable easy flows of electronic data. Alongside the offshore world Cameron and Palan (2004) identify the salience of ideas of the transformed 'national economy' (ideas akin to those put forward by the transformationalists such as Cerny). As noted already, this national economic space has been transformed considerably through ideas of 'no alternative' to the rising tide of globalization. Finally, they identify a third imagined economy – that of 'social exclusion', a set of ideas that concern the way in which groups within societies have been excluded and marginalized from globalization. The important point here is that these three economies have been 'imagined' – they are in a sense myths – but they are powerful myths/imaginings, they have played a significant role in shaping the world in which we live today.

What writings such as these point to is that globalization is not a singular, universal or uniform process. The problem with viewing globalizing as a uniform and all encompassing process is highlighted by Germain (2000a) who argues that views of globalization as inevitable and as something that gradually pervades every aspect of human activity are misguided. By contrast, Germain (2000b) calls for a 'historical perspective' whereby we examine how globalization comes to be set within multiple contexts throughout history. This is important because, as Rosenberg (2000) points out, first wave scholarship has a tendency to view globalization as a historical given – as something that 'explains the changing character of the modern world', ignoring the way in which globalization is 'the developing outcome of some historical process' (Rosenberg 2000: 3). A historical perspective, first, forces us to think critically about how the social practices that we engage in have created globalized spaces (such as Cameron and Palan's 'offshore' world). Second, an acceptance that globalization is not a historical given, an inevitable process, also opens up spaces for challenging and confronting globalization – an issue that we now turn to discuss.

CHALLENGING GLOBALIZATION

The strength of the third wave scholarship, therefore, is the recognition that powerful discursive and ideological constructions have played a role in shaping ideas of globalization. The argument therefore follows that in identifying these power relations we are able to build a basis upon which dominant (in particular neo-liberal economic) ideas of globalization can be resisted and challenged. Challenging globalization, argue Chin and Mittleman (1997), needs to be located within an analysis of the role of power in shaping what we think we 'know' about globalization. Central to this focus on resistance therefore, is a refutation of the hyperglobalization or business globalization literature whereby an overtly economistic view of globalization is presented as a route to prosperity and progress.

Intellectual challenges to mainstream globalization discourse, often employ an argument that identifies globalization with neo-liberalism (Gills 2000: 4). In this view globalization is presented as a commitment to neo-liberal capitalism pursued in the interests of the powerful (the richer nations and classes of people) at the expense of the weak and the poor. Such challenges can be backed with the presentation of statistics on the widening of global poverty. For example, the United Nation's 2003 *Human Development Report* says that during the booming 1990s, 54 poor countries actually got poorer in terms of how they measured on the Human Development Index (a bundle of measures that includes things like infant mortality rates, levels of educational attainment and access to clean water) (UNDP 2003). So despite the claim of the neo-liberals that globalization is a force for prosperity and progress, many people around the world remain sceptical about the extent to which a global economic system built upon neo-liberal capitalist principles can bring benefits to all peoples of the world.

The most obvious manifestation of these concerns is in the so-called anti-globalization movement (see Box 7.1) which is a term that is often given to the loose networks of campaigners who have sought to protest about the negative consequences of economic

BOX 7.1 THE ANTI-GLOBALIZATION MOVEMENT

A discussion of resistances to globalization would be incomplete without looking at the so-called 'anti-globalization' movement. This is a term that is often applied to the groups and networks of campaigners who seek to challenge the dominance of neo-liberal economic ideas in global politics and what they see as a multinational corporate driven global capitalism. The term 'anti-globalization' is rather misleading – after all the movement is often viewed as a product of globalization; making use of the technological innovations in transport and communication technologies to network and spread their messages and ideas around the world. Given the problematic nature of the term anti-globalization, then, you will probably also come across terms such as the anti-capitalist movement, the global resistance movement and the global justice movement – among other labels. For writers such as Richard Falk (2000), the emergence of these anti-corporate globalization protesters is representative of a 'globalization from below'. Others utilize ideas of 'global civil society' to explain the various networks of anti-globalization activists.

The emergence of an anti-globalization movement is overwhelmingly linked to the 1999 'Battle for Seattle' in which vast networks of protestors convened on the city of Seattle to protest at a meeting of the WTO. The protests brought together a wide array of different kinds of groups, organizations and individuals – steelworkers, students, trade unions, environmentalists, women's groups, anarchists, local citizens and many others in protest at what they saw to be the injustice of an emerging neo-liberal economic global order. WTO, G8, IMF and World Economic Forum meetings have been the particular target of these campaigns because they are viewed as representative of the institutions that shore up a global economic system based upon neo-liberal economic principles. While the various groups involved in these protests are very diverse, at some level they all share a concern that a neo-liberal economic system does not deliver progress and prosperity but inequality and injustice.

Public intellectuals such as Noam Chomsky and Naomi Klein (the author of the influential book *No Logo*, 2001) are often linked to an anti-globalization movement. Also associated with it is the 1994 Zapatista rebellion in the Chiapas region of Mexico. The rebellion which took place on the same date as the signing of the North American Free Trade Agreement (NAFTA) which established a free trade zone between Canada, the United States and Mexico is also often depicted as part of a globalized politics of resistance to institutions (such as NAFTA) that are viewed as supporting neo-liberalism.

There is debate over the extent to which 'anti-globalization' activities can really be labelled a 'movement' at all. After all it constitutes a wide and diverse network of activists with quite diverse, and often conflicting, goals (Eschle 2005). The emergence of the World Social Forums from 2001 onwards has been one of the most interesting developments in terms of global resistance politics. These annual forums, which are linked to a number of regional and local sub-forums, have provided a space for debating, discussing issues relating to neo-liberal globalization and forging strategies of resistance.

globalization and the dominance of neo-liberal economic institutions such as the World Bank, the IMF and the WTO. These institutions are equated with shoring up an economic system that benefits the wealthy at the expense of the poor. For example, for many years the IMF and the World Bank have pursued policies of structural adjustment that have forced states in the developing world to cut welfare spending in favour of debt repayment and open up their economies to market forces through policies of deregulation and privatization. While the IMF and World Bank argue that these are policies that will, ultimately, bring prosperity to developing nations, critics have suggested that they have actually contributed to the worsening levels of global inequality and poverty noted in the *Human Development Report*. Of course, as we reflect in Box 7.1, the idea of an anti-globalization movement is itself highly prob-lematic and something of a contested concept.

We can therefore point to the emergence of some sort of global social movement committed to challenging neo-liberal global capital as part of the challenge to the discursive hegemony of 'business globalization'. Amoore *et al.* (1997) have suggested:

> Resistance groups should act to break down the myth, which is often perpetrated by governments, that they are helpless in the face of globalization, and refuse to accept that their own hands are tied by the inevitable onrush of global economic forces.
>
> (Amoore *et al.* 1997: 193)

But more than this, we can also point to the role of academic scholarship in helping to develop critiques of global capitalism. An important strand of scholarship that identifies globalization with inequality and injustice comes from feminism. Concerns have been raised for example about the impact of structural adjustment on women in the developing world (Rai 2002) and about the low wages and exploitative working conditions that largely female workforces experience in 'global factories' around the world (Elson and Pearson 1981). These exploitative working conditions are often a reflection of the widely held idea that women are mere 'secondary' workers – working to supplement a male 'breadwinner's' wages. Many feminists suggest, therefore, that we need to think about how assumptions that women belong to an essentially 'reproductive' sphere underpin mainstream globalization discourses (Peterson 2003). It is perhaps unsurprising then, given the highly gendered effects of economic globalization, that women's movements have played a significant role within the so-called anti-globalization movement.

Some third wave globalization scholars concerned with the politics of resistance have invoked a 'historical perspective' drawing upon the work of scholars such as Antonio Gramsci and Karl Polanyi who, in the early to mid twentieth century, sought to conceptualize resistance to (global) capital (Chin and Mittleman 1997). Robert Cox, for example, drawing upon Gramsci's work has written of the possibilities for counter-hegemonic resistance to a global capitalist hegemony (Cox 1983). Karl Polanyi's notions of counter-movement invoke the idea that human society is ultimately unable to deal with the social dislocation caused by capitalist transformation and this inevitably leads to resistances as people move to protect themselves from the harsh effects of the global market economy (Polanyi 1957).

What this discussion of resistance demonstrates is that globalization, however we might understand it, raises important normative issues for the student of IR. In particular questions of poverty (and to a lesser extent, gender inequality) are now inextricably mixed up with debates around globalization. This concern with the negative impacts of globalization and the ethical dilemmas that globalization poses for the world is largely the result of the fact that people have dared to be critical of existing understandings of globalization. In the final chapter of this book, we focus in more depth on the current ethical and moral issues facing the world. This is a discussion that cannot take place without taking into account the massive changes in world politics that we associate with globalization. In this sense, while this chapter has focused on how notions of globalization have changed our understanding of global politics, Chapter 8 will consider how normative theory and theorizing in IR has confronted the issue of globalization (as well as other contemporary issues in world politics).

TOPICS FOR DISCUSSION

1 What is international political economy (IPE)? What are the major theoretical traditions of IPE scholarship?
2 What kinds of processes and changes are conventionally associated with 'globalization'?
3 How might we conceptualize the relationship between globalization and the state?
4 Do you agree or disagree with the 'hyperglobalization' thesis?
5 Who are the main 'winners' and 'losers' in the contemporary global political economy?
6 Is it possible to talk of an 'anti-globalization' movement?

FURTHER READINGS:

IPE

O'Brien, R. and Williams, M. (2004) *Global Political Economy: Evolution and Dynamics*, Basingstoke: Palgrave MacMillan.

Ravenhill, J. (ed.) (2005) *Global Political Economy*, Oxford: Oxford University Press.

Stubbs, R. and Underhill, G. (eds) (2000) *Political Economy and the Changing Global Order*, second edition, Oxford: Oxford University Press.

Gilpin, R. (1987) *The Political Economy of International Relations*, Princeton: Princeton University Press.

ECONOMIC GLOBALIZATION

Dicken, P. (2003) *Global Shift: Reshaping the Global Economic Map in the 21st Century*, London: Sage.

POLITICAL ASPECTS OF GLOBALIZATION

Ba, A.D. and Hoffman, M. (eds) (2005) *Contending Perspectives on Global Governance*, London: Routledge.

GLOBALIZATION: OVERVIEWS OF THE FIELD

Rosenberg, J. (2000) *The Follies of Globalisation Theory: Polemical Essays*, London.

Scholte, J.A. (2005) *Globalisation: A Critical Introduction*, second edition, Basingstoke: Palgrave MacMillan.

Bruff, I. (2005) 'Making sense of the globalisation debate when engaging in political economy analysis', *British Journal of Politics and International Relations* 7(2): 261–280.

'HYPERGLOBALIZATION'

Ohmae, K. (1999) *The Borderless World: Power and Strategy in the Interlinked Economy*, revised edition, London: Collins.

GLOBALIZATION AS 'TRANSFORMATION'

Cerny, P. (1990) *The Changing Architecture of Politics: Structure, Agency and the Future of the State*, London: Sage.

Strange, S. (1994a) *States and Markets*, second edition, London: Pinter.

'SCEPTICAL' APPROACHES TO GLOBLIZATION

Hirst, P. and Thompson, G. (1999) *Globalisation in Question: The International Economy and the Possibilities of Governance*, second edition, Cambridge: Polity Press.

SOCIAL CONSTRUCTIVIST APPROACHES

Cameron, A. and Palan, R. (2004) *The Imagined Economies of Globalisation*, London: Sage.

GLOBAL RESISTANCE

Amoore, L. (ed.) (2005) *The Global Resistance Reader*, London: Routledge.

Eschle, C. and Maiguashca, B. (2005) *Critical Theories, International Relations and 'the Anti-Globalisation Movement'*, London: Routledge.

Gills, B. (ed.) (2000) *Globalisation and the Politics of Resistance*, Basingstoke: Palgrave, pp. 46–56.

GENDER AND GLOBALIZATION

Peterson, S.V. (2003) *A Critical Rewriting of Global Political Economy: Integrating Reproductive, Productive and Virtual Economies*, London: Routledge.

Connell, R.W. (2005) 'Globalisation, Imperialism and Masculinities', in M.S. Kimmel, J. Hearn and R.W. Connell (eds) *The Handbook of Studies on Men and Masculinities*, London: Sage, pp. 71–89.

8

FROM STABILITY TO JUSTICE?

Contemporary challenges in international relations

The challenges that face the world in the new millennium are incredible. In this chapter we shall look at two central features of contemporary world affairs. We shall explore how developments in the use of military force and in economic and social development policy display a real tension in the way the world has reacted to processes associated with globalization. On the one hand, there is a clear political consensus on the need to develop global governance, international law and national policy to reflect a multilateral response to threats to what is commonly called human security. On the other is an equally clear resistance to the dilution of national sovereignty that this necessarily implies. To attempt a survey of the key developments in the way the 'international community' (or at least specific states within it) deploys its armed forces or creates economic development policy is too large an undertaking for an introduction to IR. The way that we have chosen to introduce you to the basics of these developments is to frame the issue by looking at two key issues in contemporary world politics. The first issue concerns the proper use of force in world politics. There have been rules concerning when it is right to resort to warfare for millennia and there have also been rules about how combatants should conduct themselves on the field of battle and when dealing with defeated enemies, their territory and civilians. However, the permissiveness of these rules (and the rather lax way they were translated into practice) would surprise the new reader. Most of the changes to the rules concerning the use of force have been attempts to keep up with the practices of great powers or the ever advancing technology of warfare. However the rapid development of our political understanding of the place of military force in international relations and the similarly rapid development of public international law concerning the use of force since 1945 suggests a very considerable and continuing change in the attitude of the international community to what has often been considered the key policy instrument of international politics. The second issue we explore is the question of global economic justice. Calls to end poverty in the developing world have a high profile in contemporary international relations. It is a cause supported by celebrities (in contexts such as Live Aid, Live 8, Make Poverty History or Comic Relief) and one that is constantly discussed at the highest level in the UN and at G8 summits. Here we explore the progress that has been made towards meeting the demands of global economic justice and look at arguments that suggest that supporting poverty relief in the developing world is not a matter of giving charitable donations but a matter of justice and morality that is essential to the political stability of global politics.

BEYOND WESTPHALIA

At the core of both of these issues is a fierce debate about the future of international politics. Often the protagonists are caught in two minds. Most state actors are clear that there is a real need for a formal procedure that would allow the international community to engage in humanitarian intervention. Yet few are willing either to give the UN the power necessary to formalize such a procedure or to create the legal rules necessary to establish a right to intervene. Exploring this dilemma really offers us a sense of the crossroads that the international community is faced with. Similarly there is near universal acknowledgement that poverty in the developing world is not merely a matter of 'bad luck' but a problem that the international community must address. Yet once again we find that few are willing to either acknowledge the centrality of global poverty to the question of global justice or to deliver on the myriad of promises made at grand summits of the leaders of the world's wealthiest nations.

The question we intend to leave you with in this final chapter is not one that we expect you to answer right now. Rather it is one that you should think about throughout your academic career as students of IR and beyond. It is a question that can be put in any number of ways to suit any number of contexts. In this chapter we ask you to consider the following idea. Is the pressure on the international community to deliver justice on a global scale such that we should consider the state-centric 'Westphalian model' of international politics a thing of the past? You will come across this claim a lot in contemporary IR debates. It is not a claim that the nation-state is actually disappearing as a form of political community (much as the ancient Greek *poleis* or city states once disappeared). That would be too premature. Rather it is an argument that combines the following:

- *A factual claim* – sovereign states are no longer autonomous in the way that they have been since Westphalia in that there are real limits to how a state can act internally and on the use of force as a tool of foreign policy.
- *A political claim* – sovereign states are no longer the best way to manage those things that we believe to be the most important social challenges we face and so we need to imagine new political spaces that are global, regional and subnational.
- *A normative claim* – we ought to (we have good moral and political reasons to) dramatically reorganize global politics to move beyond the states system.

Ultimately arguments of this sort, if they prove to be realistic, challenge us to develop new ways of thinking about the nature of IR and to imagine new structures of global governance. To approach this question is to consider the very nature of IR and your considered opinion on this question may well structure your own outlook on all of the many questions of world politics that you will study.

RESTRICTIONS ON THE USE OF FORCE: JUST WAR AND HUMANITARIAN INTERVENTION

The Westphalian model of IR is often described in realist terms. However, when we are thinking about the place of war in the history of international politics it may be that we need to go beyond realism to think about a more extreme approach known as martialism (Nabulsi 1999). Realists do think about security in terms of military strength and they do accept the inevitability of war as a consequence of balance of power politics or the quite proper pursuit of national interest. For realists any attempt to judge warfare by universal moral standards is misguided. The attitude to war is one that sees it as necessary. The martialist tradition, by contrast, revels in and glorifies the virtues of war and sees it as the culmination of struggle towards one's destiny (Nabulsi 1999: 80, 92). The warrior code of martialism and the *machtpolitik* (power politics) of realism are very important approaches to warfare or the use of force in international politics. However, the just war tradition has an equally important place in the history of international relations. Great writers such as St Augustine in the fourth century, St Thomas Aquinas in the thirteenth century, Hugo Grotius in the seventeenth century and Michael Walzer in the twentieth century have all explored war in terms of whether it is legitimate and whether it is conducted with the proper restraint. In the language of this influential tradition we are asked to consider questions of *'Jus ad Bellum'* or when it is legitimate to resort to war and questions of *'Jus in Bello'* or how, once war is justified, we may conduct that conflict – typically questions about who we may target and the weaponry we may use. The just war tradition is not a pacifist tradition. Rather, it is a series of conventions that apply to war between similar adversaries who wish to return to business as usual after the conflict has resolved whatever issue is at stake. Just war theory does not rule out the use of force but places some limits on its employment. Nevertheless it has provided us with the tools to condemn unjust wars and acts of military barbarity and forms a strong set of moral norms at the heart of much thinking about conflict. The conventions range from specifying the person or body who can legitimately declare war to how one should treat non-combatants or prisoners of war. The important thing about this tradition is that war is to be considered in moral terms such as the just nature of its cause or the proportionality of its response. Initially the ethical component of the tradition was firmly rooted in religious values but, while this is still the case in some strands of the tradition, the principles of just war theory have become progressively embedded in international law and secular political thought. Martialism and realism are powerful voices in the historical debates concerning warfare but so are the proponents of just warfare tied up, as they have been, with powerful institutions such as the Catholic Church and, more recently, the UN.

Just war theory has developed incrementally and in response to practical necessity. The key triggers that reinvigorated debate about the ethics of war in the contemporary era include the ability to deliver devastating blows to civilian populations (from the aerial bombing campaigns of the second world war to the potential to deliver nuclear warheads), the suffering of the wounded and prisoners of war in large scale conflicts, advances in chemical weapons technology, the Holocaust and the horrors of two world wars and, more recently, the Cold War and the secessionist wars that followed its thaw. The most important component of the reinvigoration of the just war tradition has been the remarkable development of a human rights culture in international politics. The twin aims of the UN are the promotion of peace and human rights. These core values prohibit the use or threat of force (article 2.4) and pledge members to 'cooperation in solving international problems of an economic, social, cultural, or humanitarian character, and in promoting and encouraging respect for human rights and for fundamental freedoms' (article 1.3). Both of these goals are remarkable ambitions for a Westphalian system. As we shall see, despite this bold declaration, the politics of implementing the values of the post-1945 world order are fraught with tensions. These vital political developments impact on the debates concerning the use of force in two distinct ways. The first is that the central question of just war theory (under what conditions can a state go to war) has regained an importance that it lost during the eighteenth and nineteenth centuries (Rengger 2002: 356). The second is a running together of military action and humanitarianism. More and more the answer to the question 'when can a state legitimately use military force' is either in self-defence or in response to a serious humanitarian crisis. Much to the annoyance of realists (who view this development as both misguided and analytically woolly) security is now often thought of in the much broader terms of 'human security' rather than in the much narrower terms of military security. Human security is a term that brings economic and development issues together with military and security issues. It is a commonplace but much contested term. It is commonplace because it has become a part of the language of IR following the publication of the United Nations Development Programme *Human Development Report* in 1994. Since this report the idea has become firmly established in the UN where the Human Security Unit of the Office for the Coordination of Humanitarian Affairs (UNOCHA) is tasked with placing human security at the heart of UN policy. Its success can be seen in the work of the UN and its agencies, in the agenda of the Human Security Network, as well as in the policy debates among the G8 and regional organizations such as the European Union and the African Union. In academic research and debate the term human security has found a place in all schools of thought as realists, liberals, critical theorists and constructivists all seek clearer definitions and ways to measure data relating to human security in order to generate policy related research plans.

UNOCHA defines human security in the following way:

> Human security is far more than the absence of violent conflict. It encompasses human rights, good governance and access to economic opportunity, education and health care. It is a concept that comprehensively addresses both 'freedom from fear' and 'freedom from want'.

> http://ochaonline.un.org

This development is premised on the idea that traditional threats to national security – the prospect of great power war – has diminished while threats such as terrorism, poverty, disease, natural and human-made disaster have increased. In very broad terms it suggests that threats to human security require a significant development in the way we approach international politics. Force is no longer 'a continuation of politics', as Clausewitz (1968) famously put it. Rather it is one tool available to us in our search for human security.

At least this is how it sometimes appears to be. Despite there being broad agreement in public declarations on the deployment of military forces to enforce economic embargoes, protect humanitarian aid supply lines or to defend civilian populations from the horrors of civil war and inter-state conflict the political and legal machinery necessary to effect his transition lags behind the good intentions of the principal agents. The reason for this is simple. The principles of humanitarianism are in conflict with principles of sovereignty and a strong international legal regime and a strong UN capable of delivering on the principles of humanitarianism represents a real threat to sovereignty.

HUMANITARIAN INTERVENTION AND INTERNATIONAL LAW

The actors seem to be in two minds about the issue. On the one hand, there was never any intention to develop a regime of humanitarian intervention when the UN was established. Under Chapter VII of the charter the Security Council had powers of forcible intervention when it determined that a conflict constituted a threat to international peace and security (article 42). Note the phrase 'international' peace. Force used by a government to quell internal unrest was still considered a domestic matter beyond the purview of the international community (Cassese 2001: 282). Nevertheless it is clear that the Security Council has gradually established a link between humanitarian crises and threats to peace (Cassese 2001: 297). Clear examples of this can be seen in operations in the former Yugoslavia (1992–1993), Rwanda (1994), Haiti (1994) and Somalia (1992). However, these operations are often criticized either for being too late (thanks to the reluctance of the Security Council to act) or for supplying an ineffective mandate to the forces on the ground. The reason for this is the desire of the members of the Security Council, and the sovereign states they represent, to retain a significant degree of discretion in the authorization regime of humanitarian intervention.

The International Law Commission of the UN, the International Court of Justice, countless fact finding reports and speeches have all played with the idea of giving humanitarian crises a special status in IR. The idea is that certain gross abuses of human rights (genocide and other crimes against humanity as well as war crimes) would require a swift response on behalf of the UN and its member states. The legal term for this special status is *Jus Cogens*. This is a term which identifies the most important norms of international law. These norms are considered to be so important that states have no choice but to conform to their principles and, unlike most international law, are not the product of state consent. This would, of course, eliminate the degree of discretion that member states currently have in relation to humanitarian intervention and make the UN much more efficient in dealing with these large scale human disasters. Yet despite the evolution of the language of *Jus Cogens*, broad agreement that humanitarian crises and war crimes come under this heading and a reasonably consistent pattern of humanitarian interventions being authorised by the Security Council the whole regime remains in a state of potential readiness rather than being firmly established (Cassese 2001: 138–148). This is primarily because a regime of humanitarian intervention is in opposition to the UN charter. The UN was established by the then great powers and, so some argue, its greatest strength lies in remaining a forum for the interaction of sovereign states. An established right of humanitarian intervention clearly threatens the idea of sovereignty. Establishing a codified system of humanitarian intervention would require a fresh look at the UN charter and most states (in the powerful west and in the developing world) are unwilling to waive the protections that sovereignty affords them. It seems then, that we have a situation in which the principles of humanitarian intervention are settled but where the political mechanisms are not. We know we have obligations to prevent genocide and war crimes and this is an incredible advance in the development of a universal account of global justice. But despite an informal and relatively successful series of interventions the political infrastructure is such that interventions are often a little haphazard, selective or so late as to be rather ineffective. In order to get a better understanding of this relatively new phenomenon let us look in a little more detail at the case of Darfur.

HUMANITARIAN INTERVENTION IN DARFUR

The issue of humanitarian intervention is usually discussed in terms of the grounds on which the sovereignty of a nation-state can be breached in order to protect the lives and uphold the human rights of people residing within that state. In this sense, the issue of humanitarian intervention concerns two conflicting sets of norms that are enshrined in international law. First, we can point to norms relating to state sovereignty and that sovereign states should not be subject to outside interference in their internal affairs (ideas that are upheld in article 2 of the United Nations charter). However, the attachment in international law and international relations more generally to the concept of sovereignty clearly conflicts with another group of norms relating to universalized notions of human rights – in particular the human rights set out in the 1948 Universal Declaration of Human Rights (UDHR). While the UDHR in certain respects upholds the principle of sovereignty (because it is individual states that are entrusted with the enforcement of these human rights standards) there are, obviously, problems when states turn against their own people and commit acts of gross human rights violation such as mass rape, torture, and even genocide.

The Darfur region, located in the west of the African state of Sudan, is one such area of the world in which numerous calls for humanitarian intervention have been made. The current humanitarian crisis in Sudan is largely driven by government aerial bombardment backed by an Arab militia, the *Janjaweed*, recruited locally and armed by the government. The situation in Darfur has been described as 'a massive humanitarian crisis', 'ethnic cleansing' and 'genocide'. The Government of Sudan and the Janjaweed have been responsible for gross violations of human rights against the black African population of the region.

> Since early 2003, the world has watched with both shock and apathy as Sudan's Arab-dominated government ethnically cleanses its vast western region of Darfur by arming, encouraging, and even giving air support to mostly Arab militia who kill, maim, rape, and rob black Africans. The Darfur crisis combines the worst of everything: armed conflict, extreme violence, sexual assault, great tides of desperate refugees.
>
> (Udombana 2005: 1149–1150)

As the author of the above quotation correctly points out, the crisis in Darfur has not led to a coordinated international response.

Diplomatic pressure has been placed on the Government of Sudan – for example, the Security Council has passed resolutions that have condemned the actions of the Sudanese government in the region. However, such resolutions have not been backed with commitments to take action against the Sudanese government if it continues to be involved in the atrocities. From a realist perspective, the inaction of the international community is easily explained – states will not intervene in a state unless it affects their national interest. For example, the USA's reluctance to intervene in Rwanda in the mid 1990s has been explained by pointing to the failure of the USA's attempt to intervene in the humanitarian crisis in Somalia in the early 1990s – in many respects these concerns still shade US military policy towards Africa. However, supporters of humanitarian intervention in Sudan appeal to internationally held norms relating to human rights in arguing that 'Darfur might be a complex crisis politically, but it is morally and legally simple' (Udombana 2005: 1190). Humanitarian intervention is not only viewed as a moral imperative, it is also seen as the only way to solve the current crisis – ending the killings, sending a clear message to the Government of Sudan and providing security to humanitarian assistance workers involved in essential relief work in the region; it would also enable the prosecution of those individuals who have been identified as war criminals.

As the above comments concerning Darfur indicate, the issue of humanitarian intervention is a highly contested issue. As we have seen, there is a hard-line realist position that argues that these 'moral issues' have no place in the harsh reality of international politics – intervention in the sovereign affairs of another state should only ever be justified on the grounds of national interest. Within the English school of international relations the issue of humanitarian intervention has generated considerable debate. As we saw in Chapter 4 the English school has two wings. On the one hand, a pluralist position has put forward the view that humanitarian intervention violates the norms of state sovereignty that are crucial to maintaining order within an international society of states. Essentially, pluralists argue that the key normative basis of international order (i.e. stability) is a shared commitment among states to norms of non-intervention in the sovereign affairs of other states. On the other hand, a solidarist perspective has put forward a defence of humanitarian intervention. The solidarist position is an interesting one, because it rests upon an understanding that norms change over time. Hence in the late nineteenth and early twentieth centuries it was generally the case that a commitment by other states to upholding and respecting norms of non-intervention and sovereignty was viewed as a crucial element of maintaining order in international politics (the line taken by the pluralists). However, in the late twentieth and early twenty-first centuries, states have come to place much greater emphasis on the norms surrounding human rights and justice. Wheeler (2000) thus introduces the idea of the 'supreme humanitarian emergency' – the circumstances under which states will abandon norms of non-intervention in favour of a concern with the human rights of the individual citizens of that country. Clearly the current situation in Darfur would fit within Wheeler's definition of a supreme humanitarian emergency.

> Supreme humanitarian emergencies are extraordinary situations where civilians in another state are in imminent danger of losing their life or facing appalling hardship, and where indigenous forces cannot be relied on to end these violations of human rights.
>
> (Wheeler, 2000: 50)

For authors such as Alex Bellamy (2003), however, the issue of humanitarian intervention is far more complex than debates over the grounds whereby a violation of state sovereignty is justified. The implication of arguments such as Wheeler's is that the international community has a responsibility to protect citizens in a particular state only in the very worst and most extreme cases. This position is somewhat problematic because it obscures the extent to which the great majority of suffering in the world today is not due so much to the actions of a few violent and repressive regimes – but is more likely to be the result of extreme poverty. Bellamy (2003) argues that more focus needs to be placed on the role of Western nations in supporting a global economic system that significantly disadvantages the poor. Poverty and inequality are often major contributing factors in conflict-ridden societies, and thus the argument is made for a wider focus on the idea of 'human security' – an approach to security that incorporates a concern with economic and social justice in ensuring the personal security of individuals.

THE UN AND LEGITIMATE INTERVENTION

We will explore the idea of global economic justice further in the next section. Here, however, we should reflect on two of the solidarist claims. The first is that norms change over time. As we have seen much contemporary IR theory explores the development and role of norms in world politics and this reflects the arguments that we can see in the UN Security Council, General Assembly and in the proceedings of the International Court of Justice. There is a groundswell of opinion that argues that the charter of the UN (a symbol of the attitude of the international community) is a living document that has been interpreted and reinterpreted to broaden the understanding of the proper use of force and our commitment to international justice more generally. Yet because the international legal regime relating to humanitarian intervention is what lawyers call *lex ferenda* (law as it ought to be or norms in the process of becoming law) rather than fully established *lex lata* it is not the case that we can point to the inaction of the UN in times of crisis and say categorically that member states are failing to live up to their international obligations. Rather we have to find ways to show why we think that humanitarian intervention ought to be a priority for the Security Council and convince those who have no national interest in such operations that they should get involved or, at the very least, not frustrate the decision-making mechanisms of the Security Council by exercising a veto. The solidarist position links constructivism and just war theory, the new and the old, to present us with an understanding of the evolution of norms concerning humanitarian intervention as a response to 'supreme emergency' conditions such as genocide, mass murder and ethnic cleansing that have been at the forefront of international ethics since the Second World War. Here the core idea is that stability requires justice rather than military might arranged in a balance of power.

The second claim we need to reflect upon is the solidarist claim that authorization of an intervention by the UN, in particular the Security Council, is essential to the legitimacy of that intervention.

For some scholars the moral obligation to help those confronted the unimaginable suffering occasioned by civil wars and tyrannical regimes, once established, becomes the most important issue. In his book *Justice, Legitimacy and Self-Determination: The Moral Foundations of International Law*, Allen Buchanan (2004) argues that the obvious conflict between principles of humanitarian intervention and the national self-interest of sovereign states requires a complete rejection of the 'UN-based law of humanitarian intervention' and of the 'state-consent model of international law' more generally (Buchanan 2004: 1–14). The argument is clear. If you have principles of justice that oblige us to aid those in extreme suffering but political and legal institutions that are structurally unable to deliver on those obligations then we need to reform or scrap those institutions. The structure of the UN charter and the Security Council is such that instances of humanitarian disaster are dealt with late, or selectively, if at all and the prospects for constitutional reform are bleak. It therefore stands to reason that we need to move beyond the UN and the system of international law that gives sovereign actors the freedom to be above the law. However, for Wheeler (2000) and the solidarists, we must recognize that the development of norms of humanitarian intervention is 'subject to the very important caveat that the society of states shows little or no enthusiasm for legitimating acts of humanitarian intervention not authorized by the Security Council' (Wheeler 2000: 286). In other words we are constrained by a genuine reluctance to give up the rights and protections of sovereignty. How should you decide which position to adopt (and these are not the only possible positions)? Ultimately it will require that you engage with the political, legal and moral arguments that constitute IR theory. It is not really a matter of finding the 'truth' of the matter. Rather it is a matter of becoming informed enough to add your voice to the diplomatic dialogue that ultimately shapes the development of our international political system.

WORLD POVERTY AND GLOBAL ECONOMIC JUSTICE: MILLENNIUM DEVELOPMENT GOALS

The idea that only justice will bring genuine stability has a long history. But it does rather beg the question 'What is justice?', which has an even longer history. For a long time mainstream IR sought to avoid the question, regarding it as masking the real questions concerning power relations. But the post-1945 world has proven an increasingly fertile arena for exploring questions of international justice and a lot of effort and money has gone in to trying to meet the demands that this places upon the international community.

MILLENNIUM DEVELOPMENT GOALS AND GLOBAL POVERTY

One large scale example of this can be seen in the construction of the development goals of the UN. The dawn of a new millennium provided, in the words of the Secretary General Kofi Annan, the opportunity for the peoples of the world under the auspices of the UN 'to reflect on their common destiny at a moment when they find themselves interconnected as never before' (A/54/200). At the Millennium Summit held in New York in September 2000, 189 nations adopted the UN General Assembly resolution 55/2 the 'Millennium Declaration'. This resolution provided the basis for political cooperation towards eight millennium development goals (MDGs). These are as follows:

Goal 1: Eradicate extreme poverty and hunger
Goal 2: Achieve universal primary education
Goal 3: Promote gender equality and empower women
Goal 4: Reduce child mortality
Goal 5: Improve maternal health
Goal 6: Combat HIV/AIDS, malaria and other diseases
Goal 7: Ensure environmental sustainability
Goal 8: Develop a Global Partnership for Development

These goals were to be met by 2015. The millennium development goals are far more than wordy declarations. They are time-specific, measurable and enjoy immense political support. Yet the progress towards these goals in the millennium development goals report 2005 did not make encouraging reading. All of these goals are immensely important and represent vital challenges for the international community but to get a sense of the scale of the problem, the approach to tackling the issues and the progress to date we shall focus solely on poverty and child mortality.

The headline target we are interested in is the eradication of extreme poverty and hunger. The MDG is to halve, by 2015, the number of people living on less than $1 a day. While this goal includes all people and not just children, we can get some idea of the enormity of this problem from two pieces of data. The first is that more than a quarter of children in the developing world are malnourished and that is around 146 million (see Figure 8.1).

Second, every year around 11 million children under the age of 5 die. That is 30,000 children a day. Child mortality is closely linked to poverty and so it is not surprising that the peoples of the United Nations sought to act. However, one third of the time we set ourselves to halve poverty has passed but while progress is being made, the MDG's report 2005 is clear that we are far from winning this vital battle (see www.childinfo.org).

In fact the problem is such that progress towards eradicating hunger is not keeping up with global population growth and it is likely that hitting the target will take more than 130 years rather

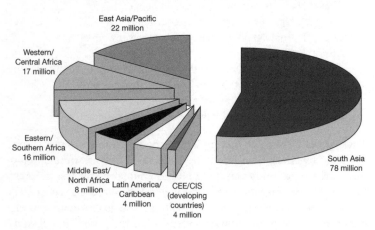

146 million children are underweight in the developing world and more than half of these children live in South Asia

Figure 8.1 Child malnutrition in the developing world

Source: UNICEF analysis of the number of underweight children in the developing world, 2006

than the 15 the UN envisaged (UNDP 2002). It is the case that while progress is made in one area, ground is being lost in another. So while it is true that the average income of the very poor in most of the developing world has increased from $0.80 a day to $0.82 a day the income of the very poorest in Sub-Saharan Africa has actually decreased from $0.62 a day to $0.60. That leads to another 34 million people having insufficient food.

The political language and effort of the UN and the global partnership for develop should not be underestimated but what is it that is preventing a reasonably united UN from hitting its targets? The problem is often characterized in similar terms to those we explored in relation to humanitarian intervention. A system of sovereign states where the priority of the actors is self-help does not seem to be the most fruitful ground for sowing the seed of global economic equity. For some political commentators our moral obligations are very clear. We are committed to human rights, to the eradication of poverty and (under article 28 of the UDHR) to the establishment of social institutions that are capable of delivering on these commitments. Yet we persistently fail to live up to these standards.

A CRITICAL APPROACH TO GLOBAL ECONOMIC JUSTICE

Cosmopolitans such as Thomas Pogge and critical thinkers such as Jan Aart Scholte see quite radical consequences following from this. For both thinkers the institutions of global capitalism from which the developed world draws so much of its wealth is the chief cause of such dire poverty and political inequality (Pogge 2002; Scholte 2005). Both argue from very different premises. Scholte (2005) targets neo-liberal economic policies favoured by powerful governments and multilateral organizations such as the International Monetary Fund, the World Trade Organization and the Organization for Economic Cooperation and Development (OECD). For Scholte the adoption of neo-liberal economic policy is to choose to opt out of the management of the inequities that arise from globalization. Indeed it is to adopt a policy that structurally encourages the emergence of a divide between rich and poor. The consequence of the dominance of neo-liberalism in economic policy may have some productivity benefits but as Scholte shows this comes at high price.

'Free markets' in supraterritorial spaces have often perpetuated or deepened ecological degradation, poverty, labour abuses, xenophobia, class and country hierarchies, democratic deficits, and other violences. Thus governance arrangements need not only to enable global capitalism, but also to harness it to serve the vulnerable as well as the advantaged.

(Scholte 2000: 286–287)

In other words the world wealthy and powerful are happy to make commitments to human security in the UN but are actively pursuing economic liberalization and thus causing the inequities that threaten human security through the very agencies through which it may be possible to address the problem. Indeed it may not be possible to achieve human security without a radical rethink of the politics and economics of global governance. Scholte's 'ambitious reformism' requires a global social democracy with real constraints on capitalist market dynamics, the end of the sovereignty principle and the institution of multilayered governance and the proper resourcing of institutions dedicated to the achievement of greater security, justice and democracy in a globalizing world (Scholte 2000: 283–317). Ultimately, Scholte argues, the achievement of human security is dependent on a post-liberal capitalist, post-territorialist, post-sovereign politics. In other words we need to completely redevelop the way we conduct our economic and political lives.

Thomas Pogge's cosmopolitan liberalism also suggests that we need to comprehensively review our moral and political commitments in the light of global economic inequality. However he presents his powerful arguments in a rather different light, proposing 'modest and feasible, but significant, global institutional reforms that would better align our international order with our moral values' (Pogge 2002: 1–2). Pogge relies on the same shocking statistics that we examined above to get his case going. He adds to this clearly regrettable fact a further argument that this state of affairs is not an unfortunate side-effect of globalization or an accident of nature but is one that we cause. We are indicted in the causal chain of world poverty by the fact that we participate in a set of global political and economic institutions that cause every bit as much harm as slavery and colonialism ever did. Indeed we benefit materially from this situation just as our slave-owning, empire-building ancestors did. To be implicated in the deaths of 30,000 children under the age of 5 every day is shocking and the moral argument that Pogge presents us with does not appear too controversial. He argues:

> Human agents are not to collaborate in upholding a coercive institutional order that avoidably restricts the freedom of some so as to render their access to basic necessities insecure without compensating for their collaboration by protecting its victims or working for its reform.
>
> (Pogge 2002: 70)

Our common allegiance to the principles of human rights provides the basic justification for this moral claim and Pogge's moral theory is distinctive in that we have moral obligations to the worlds poor not just because they are poor but because we are institutionally connected to the causes of their poverty. Yet despite the clarity of the moral issue, we are making, as we have seen, little progress. Pogge's route out of this dilemma has several strands. Like many contemporary political theorists Pogge wants 'global institutional reform with significant reductions in national sovereignty' (Pogge 2002: 195) and he offers a conceptual sketch of such a scheme. However, his work is at its most poignant when he shows how little we need to do to make a real start on delivering our promises. It would cost, Pogge argues, only 1.2 per cent of the aggregate annual gross incomes of the high income economies to overcome the shortfall between all the world poverty stricken and the $2 a day poverty line (Pogge 2002: 7). If we thought such a fall in the standard of living too great a burden for the sake of the eradication of global poverty (!) then he proposes two taxation regimes that could raise the income. The first is the Tobin tax on the 1.8 trillion dollar a day currency speculation market where a 0.1 to 0.25 per cent tax (about 10 to 25 cents per hundred dollars traded) could generate between $100 million and $300 million dollars a year without discouraging productive long-term investment. The second is a global resources dividend – a tax on the depletion and pollution of the world's natural resources. Initially we would need $300 billion (a consequence of years of inequality) but a $2 a barrel tax on crude oil alone would raise 18 per cent of this. Pogge's liberal cosmopolitanism strives for modesty in its moral argument and in its practical reforms and this is essential given the reputation for utopianism that liberal IR theory has endured. But the focus on global economic justice that Scholte's critical theory and Pogge's cosmopolitanism bring to IR theory places them firmly at the heart of urgent contemporary debates.

INTERCONNECTEDNESS AND THE FUTURE OF WORLD POLITICS

Calls for justice in international affairs are not new but they are coloured by globalization. Kofi Annan's phrase about us being 'interconnected as never before' captures the starting point for the reflection of the critical theorists, the just war theorists and the cosmopolitans very well indeed. For Wheeler, Walzer, Scholte and Pogge it is the social and political circumstances of the post-1945 world that has lead us to the unfinished project of developing norms and political institutions of global justice. The complex human rights culture that permeates our globalized world has had a remarkable impact on the political rhetoric and actions of nation-states both internally and externally. An accurate description of a sovereign state must now take account of the influence of international law and the politics of international justice. Where the positions of Wheeler and Walzer, Pogge and Scholte might have seemed utopian in the mid 1940s, we are now constantly confronted with images of suffering and cries for justice and we desperately need the intellectual and social tools to confront it. But the claim here is not that we can abandon the search for stability and instead seek justice, or that we move from realism to one of the alternative perspectives on international politics. Rather the claim is that injustice perpetuates instability and that military security is but one component in the search for human security. The further claim is that we have good reason to care about instability, not just where it threatens the peace and stability of the international community at large but where it dramatically harms the life chances and human rights of the world's poor and needy. It may be that the term 'human security' is too general, too all encompassing to be anything more than a headline or a banner under which a multitude of different projects are developed. But if we accept the idea that the struggle for human security is an essential part of global governance then the sort of questions that the student of IR has to confront expand incredibly. For one you cannot merely accept the 'fact' of sovereignty and expect the potential answers to questions of global justice to be limited by that social fact. International politics has already found a number of ways to constrain the impact of this fact on the conduct of world affairs and in so doing has created an arena in which fundamental questions of morality and justice coexist with the hard questions of economic governance, national identity, ecological survival, the development of international law as well as national and global military security. Indeed it may be the case that this process has gone so far that the calls of authors like Buchanan, Scholte and Pogge for a post-sovereign, post-Westphalian politics have to be taken very seriously. It may be that you have embarked on a course of study and the most fascinating but most complex moment in the history of the discipline.

CONCLUDING REMARKS

Whether we are looking at the debates on humanitarian intervention or global economic justice it is clear that there is intense pressure on traditional forms of global governance. However, it is also perfectly clear that despite an increasing number of constraints on the external and internal actions of sovereign states we still live in a world structured by state sovereignty. Is it possible or even desirable to resolve this tension? If not what are the consequences for international politics? If so what next? An answer to these questions is considerably beyond the scope of an introductory guide to the basic of international relations but, one way or another, searching for the answer to these questions forms the core of contemporary international studies. Your search for answers will be informed by the ideas that we have sketched out in this introduction. Your search begins with an attempt to find your own voice in the debates about how best to 'do' IR. The early decisions you make must be held permanently up to the critical scrutiny of new ideas and different points of view because in engaging with our subject you add an informed voice to the political dialogue of international relations.

TOPICS FOR DISCUSSION

1 Does the current understanding of the legitimate use of force in international affairs suggest that we have transcended the Westphalian system of international politics?
2 Why are the peoples of the UN so resistant to the establishment of a right of humanitarian intervention?
3 Why might we consider global poverty a matter of injustice rather than bad luck?
4 Does globalization herald an era of greater international justice or greater exploitation of the poor and politically weak?

FURTHER READING

Reports by bodies such as the UN and the International Commission on Intervention and State Sovereignty (ICISS) make good primary sources and you should search for information on their websites regularly. In particular you should look at the following:

ICISS (2001) *The Responsibility to Protect*, published by the International Development Research centre and available at http://www.iciss.ca/pdf/Commission-Report.pdf.

UN (2005) *The Millennium Development Goals Report 2005*, New York available at http://unstats.un.org/unsd/mi/pdf/MDG%20Book.pdf.

ON THE DEVELOPMENT OF INTERNATIONAL NORMS ON THE USE OF FORCE

Cassese, A. (2001) *International Law*, Oxford: Oxford University Press.

Wheeler, N. (2000) *Saving Strangers: Humanitarian Intervention in International Society*, Oxford: Oxford University Press.

Walzer, M. (2004) *Arguing about War*, New Haven, CT: Yale University Press.

Walzer, M. (1978) *Just and Unjust Wars: A Moral Argument with Historical Illustrations*, New York: Basic Books.

ON GLOBAL ECONOMIC JUSTICE

Scholte, J. (2005), *Globalization: A Critical Introduction*, second edition, Basingstoke: Palgrave Macmillan.

Pogge, T. (2002) *World Poverty and Human Rights: Cosmopolitan Responsibilities and Reforms*, Cambridge: Polity Press.

GLOSSARY OF KEY TERMS

Anarchy A description of the non-hierarchical politics said to be characteristic of international relations. Anarchy literally means 'the lack or absence of ruler' and is used by some international relations scholars (especially **realists**) to describe the condition in which states find themselves in international politics. The term is frequently employed to suggest that there is a fundamental difference international and domestic political life.

Balance-of-Power A common image of international relations designed to capture the constant adjustment and readjustment of the principal actors as they attempt to create a reasonably stable international system. The 'balance of power' might relate to the actual distribution of power between states (in terms of their material capabilities) but it also might be used to refer to an ideal state of stability. For some **realists** such a balance is a triumph of diplomatic manoeuvring, for others it is the inevitable consequence of rational self-interest.

Bipolarity An understanding of international relations that stresses the existence of two major centres of power (or poles). These will usually consist of a number of states who have aligned themselves to two particular powers. The **Cold War** is understood as an era marked by bipolarity. For **neo-realists** like Kenneth Waltz, bipolarity constitutes the most stable system of international relations.

Bretton Woods Institutions The collective name given to those institutions established for the purpose of managing the world economy at the 1944 Bretton Woods Conference in New Hampshire. These organizations are the World Bank (formally known as the International Bank for Reconstruction and Development) and the International Monetary Fund.

Cold War Name given to the era of international history that lasted from approximately 1947 to 1990. The Cold War era saw most of the world divided into two ideological camps allied to one of the two 'superpowers' (the USA and the USSR). It was labelled the Cold War because all-out conflict never occurred between the two powers (although there were plenty of proxy wars that took place with the support of the superpowers during this era, for example in Korea, Vietnam and Angola). The Cold War is perhaps the most obvious instance of a **bipolar** system.

Collective security States working together to ensure their common security interests. Specifically, the idea of collective security is invoked to suggest that an attack on any one member of the collective is an attack on all members of the collective and therefore subject to a collective response. Ideas of collective security underpinned the founding of the **League of Nations**, the United Nations and the North Atlantic Treaty Organization as well as many other regional security treaties.

Complex interdependence A central idea in **neo-liberal institutionalism**. The claim is that there are multiple channels of political interaction between states, **multinational corporations**, NGOs and IGOs and that a proper understanding of IR must take account of this fact.

Cosmopolitanism Most often associated with **normative** liberal theory, cosmopolitanism is committed to individualism and universalism and to the construction of a global political order in which these core values can be effectively promoted. Core among the concerns of cosmopolitans are the promotion of human rights, global economic justice and the insistence that sovereign borders are not moral boundaries.

Critical theory Primarily associated with specific strands of Marxist scholarship, critical theorists have sought to challenge the way in which 'common sense' ways of thinking act to shore up systems of social, political and economic inequality. Critical theory is often associated with the work of various **Neo-Gramscian** scholars such as Robert Cox. We have focused on these theorists in this book; however, it is also worth noting that another important strand of critical theory scholarship draws upon the work of early twentieth century philosophy associated with the Frankfurt school. Critical theory differs from **postmodernism** largely because of its Marxist roots, which give it a much greater emphasis on **emancipatory** social change.

Democratic peace thesis The empirical claim, associated primarily with Michael Doyle, that democratic states do not go to war with one another. This is often cited as one of the advantages of liberal policies. The idea of democratic peace can also be seen as early as Woodrow Wilson's attacks on autocracy and secret diplomacy in 1919. Recent Bush administration policies emphazising democracy promotion and 'regime change' also reflect notions of democratic peace.

Diaspora The term given to members of a particular national, ethnic or religious community living outside of their traditionally defined communal boundaries. For example, the term 'Italian Diaspora' is employed to describe the many thousands of people of Italian descent living around the world.

Emancipatory (as in emancipatory theory) An emancipatory theory is one that recognises that one of the goals of theory is a commitment to overthrowing an exiting social order and thereby generating positive change for (particularly oppressed) groups of people. Within IR emancipatory approaches are associated with Marxism (including the work of the **Neo-Gramscians**) and **feminism**. Emancipatory theories are therefore **normative** theories; however, not all normative theories are emancipatory theories because they lack a commitment to radical social change.

Empiricism The argument that the world consists of facts that exist independently of the observer and whose meaning and significance can be known simply by observation. Facts are therefore viewed as being out there in the 'real world' and can be studied objectively.

It can be contrasted with the emphasis on **social constructivism** that is found in much recent international relations scholarship where by the argument is made that the observer drawing upon prior experience of the world, conveys meaning on particular 'facts' on the basis of that experience.

English school theories The 'international society' approach to IR theory, often referred to as the 'English school', is characterized by its attempts to avoid the polarization seen in the debates between **realists** and **liberals** and by its commitment to the study of what Hedley Bull, one of the school's most important contributors, called 'the anarchical society'. As this term suggests, the English school approach not only recognizes that **anarchy** is a structural feature of international relations but also recognizes that **sovereign** states form a society that uses conceptions of order *and* justice in its rhetoric and its calculations. The approach thus looks at **balance of power** *and* international law, great power politics *and* the spread of **cosmopolitan** values. The great strength of the approach is its refusal to engage with the **positivist** methodological turn in IR. Rather than adopt a positivist social science approach to the study of world affairs it offers a 'methodologically pluralist' approach to IR drawing on the study of history, philosophy and law.

Epistemology The branch of philosophy that explores questions concerning the origin and authority of knowledge. In IR we ask epistemological questions right at the outset of our explorations such as 'how do we come to know the essential nature of international politics'. The answer to such basic questions can have a profound effect on your study particularly if you decide that we cannot know anything about morality and must content ourselves with studying the world scientifically.

Feminism Feminist IR scholars raise concerns about the absence of a concern with gender issues in the discipline. On the one hand, this is witnessed in the absence of women as a category and, on the other hand, in the failure to recognise how the core categories and tools of analysis employed in IR reflect gendered assumptions and biases. Feminism is, therefore, a critical **post-positivist** approach to the study of IR challenging the relationship between men, masculinity and power in the discipline. But it is also a

normative project rooted in the concerns of feminist scholarship about improving the role and position of women around the world.

Foreign direct investment When **multinational corporations** set up subsidiary operations (e.g. a factory) in another state.

Global civil society A term that is used to refer to the emerging networks of non-governmental organizations, social and protest movements that have become a feature of international politics today.

Global governance A contested term that is used to refer to the various ways in which power and authority operates at an international level. Sometimes this is allied to a critique of the way in which processes of global governance structure global systems of inequality, subordination and exploitation. For some, however, global governance concerns the study of intergovernmental organizations and how practical solutions can be found to pressing global problems (such as climate change or developing principles for **humanitarian intervention**).

Hegemony In conventional IR theory, hegemony refers to the dominance of one particular state in world politics. However, hegemony infers more than mere unipolarity, it is not just about how much power a state has, it is concerned more with the idea of influence. Hegemony is used not only to explain the dominance of a particular state but also to show the mechanisms through which that state's power is maintained. This might include imperial possessions, military capabilities, economic might, effective dominance of multilateral institutions etc. Within **Neo-Gramscian** accounts hegemony is also employed to explain how the influence of a particular state (or more specifically a set of transnational class forces) is not simply down to coercive capacity – it also reflects an ideological power. The coercive power of states committed to the expansion of a global capitalist system is therefore backed by mechanisms for engendering consent – which can include cultural forces such as the media, consumerism and individualism.

Humanitarian intervention In general terms humanitarian intervention refers to the interference in the internal affairs of a state by another state, coalition of states, regional or intergovernmental organization on humanitarian grounds. The term is often defined to refer only to the use of military force leaving other forms of intervention (economic sanctions for example) aside. The idea that there are circumstances when such interventions are legitimate has caused much debate in political, legal and scholarly circles as the idea conflicts fundamentally with the principle of **sovereignty**. Issues in the debate include whether or not the UN should formally recognise a right or duty of humanitarian intervention at all, if so what actions should render a state liable to intervention (genocide, tyranny, civil war and the breakdown of civil society are candidates here), and what responsibilities the intervening parties assume for the future of the target state.

Idealism A liberal internationalist approach to the study of IR that is viewed as emerging after the First World War. Commonly idealism is associated with the US President Woodrow Wilson. Wilson's Fourteen Points are often viewed as something of an idealist manifesto. Idealism is a term that was rarely employed by its adherents and as an approach to international relations; it was derided by the scholar E.H. Carr as 'Utopianism'.

International political economy (IPE) An approach to the study of international politics that concerns the study of the relationship between (international) politics and economics. Much IPE scholarship has focused on explaining the relationship between the state and the market (or market actors such as **multinational corporations**). IPE scholarship has focused on issues such as financial markets, **global governance** and international organizations, global firms and production, economic **regionalism** – and most significantly globalization. More recent scholarship in IPE has sought to look more at the localized impacts of global economic and political change and raises **normative** concerns about these changes. Some of the most influential scholars within IPE include Susan Strange, Robert Keohane and Robert Cox.

League of Nations An international organization established by the Treaty of Versailles (which formally concluded, in 1919, the First World War) that committed its members to the peaceful resolution of disputes and, if that failed, to a policy of collective security. The League was comprised of an executive council and an assembly that included representatives of all member states. Its headquarters were in Geneva, Switzerland.

Just War Theory Just War Theory is a political and legal tradition of thinking about armed conflict. It comprises two key elements. *Jus ad Bellum* explores the legitimacy, or otherwise, of war asking what constitutes a just cause for war and under what authority a war may be waged. A typical example of just cause would be self-defence and typical examples of proper authority would be the **sovereign** state or the UN Security Council. *Jus in Bello* explores questions relating to the just conduct of war. Issues explored here include the questions of non-combatant immunity, the proper way to treat prisoners of war and what tools may be employed (focusing, for example on the use of chemical and biological weapons, anti-personnel landmines or tactics such as the carpet bombing of industrial infrastructure). This approach is centuries old but recent additions to the literature include a greater emphasis on humanitarian crises as legitimizing armed intervention (*Jus ad Vim*) and questions of *Jus Post Bellum* which looks at just peace settlements and the social and political reconstruction of a defeated or occupied territory.

Liberalism Like **realism**, liberalism (sometimes pejoratively termed **idealism** or utopianism) is a very broad tradition comprising many distinct and often antithetical points of view. In IR textbooks liberalism is principally associated with the internationalism of inter-war liberals such as Woodrow Wilson and, more recently, with the work of **neo-liberal institutionalists** such as Robert Keohane and Joseph Nye (see Chapter 1). Liberalism is therefore described in broad terms as relying on claims about the impact of interdependence, the benefits of free trade, **collective security** and the existence of a real harmony of interests between states. In political theory or political philosophy, liberalism is explored in significantly different terms. There liberalism is presented as a set of **normative** or moral claims about the importance of individual freedoms and rights.

Lens of gender Applying the 'lens of gender' is a metaphor employed by V. Spike Peterson and Ann Sisson Runyan to demonstrate the potentially transformative capacity of **feminist** IR scholarship. Some scholars suggest that we can study women and gender using essentially the same methodologies found within mainstream IR (an approach that has been characterized as 'add women and stir'). Applying gendered lenses implies the adoption of a broader approach – one in which the main categories of analysis that we use in IR are revealed as reflecting gendered biases.

Martialism A tradition that glorifies war and military conquest and highlighted by Nabulsi (1999) as one of the central attitudes to war in post-Enlightenment Europe.

Multilateralism The idea that multiple countries can cooperate and work together in concert. **Multilateralism** is usually associated with countries working through international institutions (or multilateral institutions) such as the United Nations. The term 'multilateral system' is often employed to refer to cooperation between states working within institutionalized frameworks of cooperation such as international law and the United Nations system. Multilateralism is usually contrasted with **unilateralism**.

Multinational corporation (MNC) When firms that are based in one country establish operations such as factories or offices in another country, then that firm has gone 'multinational'. The original country is often referred to as the 'home' country and the overseas country as the 'host' country. Some MNCs are horizontally organized, meaning that all of their overseas branches replicate almost exactly what they do in the home country. Firms such as McDonald's or the retail chains K-Mart and GAP would fall into this category. Other firms are vertically organized, which means that different elements of their production process are located in different parts of the world. Many manufacturing firms in industries such as electronics, motor vehicle production and textiles and clothing fall into this category.

Mutually assured destruction (MAD) The possession of a level of nuclear capability by two adversaries, which ensures that both sides would destroy one another in the event of nuclear war. Both states therefore possess what is called 'second strike capability' (a quantity of nuclear weapons, sufficiently well protected, that would allow the state to respond in near-equal or equal measure to a surprise nuclear attack by its adversary). MAD is often related to ideas of nuclear weapons acting as a 'deterrent' and is associated with the arms race that occurred during the **Cold War** whereby both sides sought to maintain nuclear parity.

National interest Broadly this concept refers to the overall interests of a state. National interest, therefore, is more than just the interests of a particular government. However the concept of national interest is highly problematic because it rests on assumptions that we actually know what the 'nation' is and that it is possible to identify a common set of interests.

Neo-Gramscians A group of scholars who have sought to apply the work of the Italian Marxist Antonio Gramsci to the study of international politics. The work of Robert Cox has been particularly influential in the development of a Neo-Gramscian position.

Neo-liberal institutionalism An approach to both IR and **international political economy** associated with the work of scholars such as Robert Keohane and Joseph Nye. **Neo-liberal institutionalism** differs considerably from traditional liberal approaches in IR such as **idealism** because it adopts the **positivist** and structuralist methodology associated with neo-realism. Neo-liberal institutionalism shares almost all of the central tenets of **neo-realist** theory, but differs fundamentally on the role of institutions in IR. Keohane, for example, pointed to the role of formal intergovernmental institutions, **regimes** and established conventions in international politics as playing a role in mitigating the most negative effects of international **anarchy**.

Neo-realism Associated with the work of Kenneth Waltz, neo-realism dominated the study of IR during the 1970s and 1980s. Even after the **Cold War** it remains highly influential. Neo-realists adopt a structural approach – suggesting that the existence of an international system shaped by **anarchy** structures state behaviour. In this sense, Waltz differed from traditional **realists** such as Hans Morgenthau, who located the 'realist' behaviour of states within claims concerning the selfishness of human nature. In this sense, Waltz was striving for a more scientific approach to the study of IR. The emergence of neo-realism in IR is, therefore, usually associated with the rise of **positivism** within the discipline.

New medievalism An idea first popularized in the 1970s by Hedley Bull as one possible way of conceptualizing the multilayered and fragmented nature of political authority in international politics. The term has undergone something of a revival in recent years as theorists look for ways of understanding world politics in a less state-centric manner.

Normative (as in normative theory) An approach to international politics that makes claims about how the world should be.

Ontology/ontological The study of reality. At its most basic we find that every theory has its own ontology or understanding of the nature of reality. Often we find out a considerable amount from a critical examination of a theory's ontological foundation as we find that those things that are presented as 'common sense' or necessarily true are thought to be so only because of a theory's fundamental commitment to a set of ontological truths. You will be amazed at what people simply assume to be true about IR, morality or science before they embark on a scheme of study.

Positivism The application of a 'scientific' method to the study of international relations. The main features of the positivist method are, first, an insistence on the need to develop objective (unbiased) and testifiable analyses based on the study of observable, empirical data, and second, a commitment to developing explanations, and even predictions that have a direct policy relevance.

Postmodernism In international relations, postmodernists seek to apply the theoretical insights of philosophers such as Foucault and Derrida to the discipline. Postmodernism is an anti-foundationalist position, meaning that it challenges the existence of metanarratives (essentially widely accepted stories) within the discipline. In this sense postmodernism represents a critical approach to the study of IR that raises concerns about the relationship between knowledge and power.

Post-positivist international relations Those theories (including **feminism**, **postmodernism** and **critical theory**) that seek to challenge the attachment to **positivist** methods in IR. They dispute the idea that the theorist can ever be a neutral observer of social 'reality' in favour of a view encapsulated by Robert Cox when he argued 'theory is always for someone and some purpose'.

Private military companies (PMCs) Private companies that take on military functions that are traditionally controlled by the state. PMCs are often seen as a more organized form of mercenary activity. PMCs might also be involved in ostensibly non-combat roles such as providing security guards in conflict zones.

Public international law International law reflects the fact that it is constructed by a non-hierarchical system of **sovereign** states to apply to interactions between them as well as to interactions of other international actors. International law is based primarily on the consent of states and is drawn from treaties between states and customary state practise. International law has developed rapidly since the establishment of the UN but in core areas where progressive international law collides with the self-interest of states (environmental law, humanitarian law, especially in connection with the use of force, and on the prosecution of international crimes) we find a hotbed of political activity.

Realism Realism is a general term for a particular set of theoretical approaches to the study of IR. Realism has been the dominant intellectual paradigm since the 'first great debate' between realists and liberals in the inter-war period and it set the agenda for the study of IR. Realists argue for a scientific approach to the study of IR and seek empirical truths or objective laws that can explain the dynamics of world politics. Realism is divided into two principal traditions. Classical realism suggests that human nature provides the central motor of international political actions. **Neo-realists** argue that the anarchical nature of the system is what shapes the character of IR. Both traditions argue that the objective study of IR is the study of state power in an anarchical system. This focus allows them to 'cut away' utopian ideals and non-scientific generalizations that offer false hope to policy-makers and to offer predictions based on hard 'fact'.

Regimes (as in regime theory) The study of regimes is associated with **neo-liberal institutionalism**. Broadly regimes are viewed as emerging out of a common desire among states and non-state actors to find solutions to specific international problems. Typical examples of regimes that are provided in this literature include the international postal service, the nuclear materials regime overseen by the International Atomic Energy Agency (IAEA) or the international trade regime overseen by the World Trade Organization.

Regionalism A term given to the emergence of large regions as important units of analysis in IR. Regionalism in this book is used to refer to processes of political and economic integration between states that exist in close geographic proximity to one another. Regionalism is, however, also employed in discussions on closer ties between non-state actors within geographical areas (this perspective is sometimes referred to as the 'new regionalism').

Security dilemma The idea of the security dilemma is particularly relevant to realist understandings of IR. In the realist view, the existence of international **anarchy** creates insecurity and states work to protect their national interest and, thereby, their survival through things like deploying extra military forces. However, the environment of insecurity and mistrust also means that other states will always view such actions as a threat to their security. The idea of the security dilemma can be invoked to explain arms races.

Social constructivism The idea that many of the core categories that we use to explain the social world are not absolute givens, rather they reflect dominant ideas in society. An example of a constructivist argument in IR is seen in Alexander Wendt's claim that 'anarchy is what states make of it' – that states themselves construct notions of international **anarchy** that, in turn, constrains their behaviour. At a deep level this approach threatens traditional or scientific theories of international relations because it claims that we can study the development of such norms if we adopt a fundamentally non-**positivist** account of the development of social and political knowledge (see **epistemology**).

Sovereignty International politics, many argue, is given its distinct character because the primary agents of politics are sovereign states. Sovereignty is the exclusive right, often described as originating in the treaty of **Westphalia**, to have exclusive authority over a geographic area and a people and is thought to be definitive of statehood. In the 1933 Montevideo convention on the rights and duties of state (the *locus classicus* of statehood) a state is considered a legal person in international law if it satisfies four criteria: it has (1) a permanent population, (2) a defined territory, (3) a government and (4) the capacity to enter into relations with other states. Debates concerning the implications of sovereignty are the staple of IR.

Unilateralism Unlike **multilateralism**, unilateralism is when a state acts alone rather than in concert with other states.

Westphalian system Often used as shorthand for the modern states system the phrase 'Westphalian system' refers to a series of peace treaties that ended the Thirty Years War and, in so doing, introduced the principles of **sovereignty** to European IR.

REFERENCES

Acharya, A. (2001) *Constructing a Security Community in Southeast Asia: ASEAN and the Problem of Regional Order*, London: Routledge.

Adler, E. (1997) 'Seizing the Middle Ground: Constructivism in World Politics', *European Journal of International Relations*, 3 (3): 319–363.

Adler, P.A. and Adler, P. (2004) *Paradise Labourers: Hotel Work in the Global Economy*, Ithaca, NY: Cornell University Press.

Amoore, L., Dogson, R., Gills, B.K., Langley, P., Marshall, D. and Watson, I. (1997) 'Overturning "Globalisation": Resisting the Teleological and Reclaiming the "Political"', *New Political Economu* 2 (1): 179–195.

Armstrong, J.D., Lloyd, L. and Redmond, J. (2004) *International Organisation in World Politics*, third edition, Basingstoke: Palgrave Macmillan.

Ashley, R. (1984) 'The Poverty of Neorealism,' *International Organization* 38 (2): 225–286.

Ashley, R. (1988) 'Untying the Sovereign State: a Double Reading of the Anarchy Problematique', *Millennium: Journal of International Studies* 17 (2): 227–262.

Barnet, R.J. and Cavanagh, J. (1996) *Global Dreams: Imperial Corporations and the New World Order*, Englewood Cliffs, NJ: Prentice Hall.

Bellamy, A. (2003) 'Humanitarian Responsibilities and Interventionist Claims in International Society', *Review of International Studies* 29 (3): 321–340.

Bentham, J. (1996 [1789]) *An Introduction to the Principles and Morals of Legislation*, ed. J.H. Burns and H.L.A. Hart, Oxford: Clarendon Press.

Bentham, J. (1843) *Principles of International Law*, from vol. 2 of the Bowring edition of Bentham's Works, http://www.la.utexas.edu/research/poltheory/bentham/pil/index.html

Berridge, G.R. (2002) *Diplomacy: Theory and Practise*, Basingstoke: Palgrave.

Bieler, A. and Morton, A. (2003) 'Globalisation, the State and Class Struggle: a "Critical Economy" Engagement with Open Marxism', *British Journal of Politics and International Relations* 5 (4): 467–499.

Booth, K. and Dunne, T. (eds) (2002) *Worlds in Collision: Terror and the Future of Global Order*, Basingstoke: Palgrave Macmillan.

Boucher, D. (1998) *Political Theories of International Relations from Thucydides to the Present*, Oxford: Oxford University Press.

Brenner, N. (1999) 'Beyond State Centricism? Space, Territoriality, and Geographical Scale in Globalisation Studies', *Theory and Society* 28: 39–78.

Brown, C. (1999) 'Susan Strange: A Critical Appreciation', *Review of International Studies* 25 (3): 531–535.

Brown, C. (2002) *Sovereignty, Rights, and Justice: International Political Theory Today*, Cambridge: Polity Press.

Brown, C., Nardin, T. and Rengger, N. (eds) (2002) *International Relations in Political Thought: Texts from the Ancient Greeks to the First World War*, Cambridge: Cambridge University Press.

Bruff, I. (2005) 'Making sense of the globalisation debate when engaging in political economy analysis', *British Journal of Politics and International Relations*, 7 (2): 261–280.

Buchanan, A. (2004) *Justice, Legitimacy and Self-Determination: The Moral Foundations of International Law*, Oxford: Oxford University Press.

Bull, H. (1969) 'International Theory: The Case for a Classical Approach', in K. Knorr and J.N. Rosenau (eds) *Contending Approaches to International Politics*, Princeton, NJ: Princeton University Press, pp. 20–38.

Bull, H. (1995 [1977]) *The Anarchical Society: A Study of Order in World Politics*, second edition, Basingstoke: Macmillan.

Bunch, C. (1995) 'Transforming Human Rights from a Feminist Perspective', in J. Peters and A. Wolper (eds) *Women's Rights, Human Rights: International Feminist Perspectives*, London: Routledge, pp. 11–17.

Buzan, B. (2001) 'The English School: An Underexploited Resource in IR', *Review of International Studies* 27: 471–488.

Byman, D. (2005) *Deadly Connections: States that Sponsor Terrorism*. Cambridge: Cambridge University Press.

Cameron, A. and Palan, R. (2004) *The Imagined Economies of Globalization*, London: Sage.

Cammack, P. (2002) 'The Mother of All Governments: The World Bank's Matrix for Global Governance', in R. Wilkinson and S. Hughes (eds) *Global Governance: Critical Perspectives*, London: Routledge, pp. 36–53.

Carr, E.H. (1939) *The Twenty Years' Crisis 1919–1939: An Introduction to the Study of International Relations*, London: Macmillan.

Cassese, A. (2001) *International Law*, Oxford: Oxford University Press.

Castree, N., Coe, N., Ward, K. and Stammers, M. (2004) *Spaces of Work: Global Capitalism and Geographies of Labour*, London: Sage.

Cerny, P. (1990) *The Changing Architecture of Politics: Structure, Agency and the Future of the State*, London: Sage.

Cerny, P. (2000) 'Globalisation and the Restructuring of the Political Arena: Paradoxes of the Competition State', in R. Germain (ed.) *Globalization and its Critics*, Basingstoke: Palgrave Macmillan, pp. 117–138.

Chan, S. (1997) 'In Search of Democratic Peace: Problems and Promise', *International Studies Review* 41 (1): 519–91.

Checkel, J. (1997) 'International Norms and Domestic Politics: Bridging the Rationalist Constructivist Divide', *European Journal of International Relations* 3 (4): 473–495.

Chin, C. and Mittleman, J. (1997) 'Conceptualising Resistance to Globalisation', *New Political Economy* 2 (1): 25–37.

Chomsky, N. (2002) 'Who are the Global Terrorists?', in K. Booth and T. Dunne (eds) *Worlds in Collision: Terror and the Future of Global Order*, Basingstoke: Palgrave MacMillan, pp. 128–137.

Chowdhry, G. and Nair, S. (eds) (2002) *Power, Postcolonialism and International Relations: Reading Race, Gender and Class*, London: Routledge.

Clausewitz, K. (1968) *On War*, Harmondsworth: Penguin.

Cohn, C. (1987) 'Sex and Death in the Rational World of Defence Intellectuals', *Signs: Journal of Women in Culture and Society* 12 (4): 687–718.

Connell, R.W. (2005) 'Globalisation, Imperialism and Masculinities', in M. Kimmel, J. Hearn and R.W. Connell (eds) *The Handbook of Studies on Men and Masculinities,* London: Sage, pp. 71–89.

Connor, T. (2004) 'Time to Scale-up Cooperation? Trade Unions, NGOs and the International Anti-Sweatshop Movement', *Development in Practice* 14 (1–2): 61–70.

Cox, R.W. (1981) 'Social Forces, States and World Orders: Beyond International Relations Theory', *Millennium: Journal of International Studies* 10 (2): 126–155.

Cox, R.W. (1983) 'Gramsci, Hegemony and International Relations: An essay on method', *Millennium: Journal of International Studies* 12 (2): 162–175.

Cox, R.W. (1996) *Approaches to World Order*, Cambridge: Cambridge University Press.

Cox, R.W. (1999) 'Civil Society at the Turn of the Millennium: Prospects for an Alternative World Order' *Review of International Studies* 25: 3–28.

Cronin, A.K. (2002) 'Behind the Curve: Globalization and International Terrorism', *International Security* 27 (3): 30–58.

Desch, M.C. (2003) 'It is Kind to be Cruel: the Humanity of American Realism', *Review of International Studies* 29 (3): 415–426.

Dicken, P. (2003) *Global Shift: Reshaping the Global Economic Map in the 21st Century*, London: Sage.

Dicken, P., Kelly, P., Olds, K. and Yeung, H. (2001) 'Chains, Networks, Territories and Scales: Towards a Relational Framework for Analysing the Global Economy', *Global Networks: A Journal of International Affairs* 1 (2): 89–112.

Doyle, M. (1983a) 'Kant, Liberal Legacies and Foreign Affairs', *Philosophy and Public Affairs* 12 (3): 205–235.

Doyle, M. (1983b) 'Kant, Liberal Legacies and Foreign Affairs Part 2', *Philosophy and Public Affairs* 12 (4): 323–353.

Eaton, S. and Stubbs, R. (2006) 'Is ASEAN Powerful? Neo-realist Versus Constructivist Approaches to Power in Southeast Asia', *The Pacific Review* 19 (2): 135–155.

Elias, J. (2004) *Fashioning Inequality: The Multinational Corporation and Gendered Employment in a Globalizing World,* Aldershot: Ashgate.

Elson, D. and Pearson, R. (1981) 'The Subordination of Women and the Internationalization of Factory Production', in K. Young, C. Wolkowitz and R. McCullagh (eds) *Of Marriage and the Market: Women's Subordination in International Perspective,* London: CSE, pp. 18–40.

Enloe, C. (1989) *Bananas, Beaches, and Bases: Making Feminist Sense of International Relations,* London: Pandora.

Eschle, C. (2005) 'Constructing the Anti-Globalisation Movement', in C. Eschle and B. Maiguashca (eds), *Critical Theories, International Relations and 'the Anti-Globalisation Movement',* London: Routledge.

Eschle, C. and Maiguashca, B. (eds) (2005) *Critical Theories, International Relations and 'the Anti-Globalisation Movement',* London: Routledge.

Falk, R. (2000) 'Resisting "globalisation from above", through "globalisation from below"', in B. Gills (ed.) *Globalisation and the Politics of Resistance,* Basingstoke: Palgrave, pp. 46–56.

Finnemore, M. (2001) 'Exporting the English School', *Review of International Studies* 27: 509–513.

Freeman, C. (2000) *High Tech and High Heels in the Global Economy,* Durham, NC: Duke University Press.

Friedrichs, J. (2001) 'The Meaning of New Medievalism', *European Journal of International Relations* 7 (4): 475–501.

Fukuyama, F. (1992) *The End of History and the Last Man,* London: Hamish Hamilton.

Galeotti, M. (2001) 'Underworld and Upperworld: Transnational Crime and Global Society', in D. Josselin and W. Wallace (eds) *Non-state Actors in World Politics,* Basingstoke: Palgrave, pp. 203–217.

Germain, R. (2000a) 'Globalisation in Historical Perspective', in R. Germain (ed.) *Globalisation and its Critics: Perspectives from Political Economy,* Basingstoke: MacMillan, pp. 67–90.

Germain, R. (2000b) 'Introduction: Globalisation and its Critics', in R. Germain (ed.) *Globalisation and its Critics: Perspectives from Political Economy,* Basingstoke: MacMillan, pp. xiii–xx.

Giddens, A. (2000) *Runaway World: How Globalisation is Reshaping our Lives*, New York, Routledge.

Gills, B. (2000) 'Introduction: Globalisation and the Politics of Resistance', in Gills, B. (ed.) *Globalisation and the Politics of Resistance*, Basingstoke: Palgrave, pp. 3–11.

Gilpin, R. (1987) *The Political Economy of International Relations*, Princeton, NJ: Princeton University Press.

Glasius, M., Kaldor, M. and Anheier, H. (eds) (2006) *Global Civil Society 2005/6*, London: Sage.

Goldstein, J. and Keohane, R. (eds) (1993) *Ideas and Foreign Policy*, New York: Cornell University Press.

Griffiths, M. (1999) *Fifty Key Thinkers in International Relations*, London: Routledge.

Gross, L. (1948) 'The Peace of Westphalia, 1648–1948', *American Journal of International Law* 42 (1): 20–41.

Gulick, E. (1955) *Europe's Classical Balance of Power*, Ithaca, NY: Cornell University Press.

Harvey, D. (1989) *The Condition of Postmodernity*, Oxford: Blackwell.

Hay, C. (1999) *The Political Economy of New Labour: labouring under false pretences?*, Manchester: University of Manchester Press.

Hay, C. (2004) 'The normalizing role of rationalist assumptions in the institutional embedding of neoliberalism', *Economy and Society* 33 (4): 500–527.

Hay, C. and Marsh, D. (2000) 'Introduction: Demystifying Globalisation', in C. Hay and D. Marsh (eds) *Demystifying Globalisation*, Basingstoke: Palgrave MacMillan, pp. 1–17.

Held, D. and McGrew, A. (2002) *Globalisation/Anti-Globalisation*, Cambridge: Polity Press.

Held, D., McGrew, A., Goldblatt, D. and Perraton, J. (1999). *Global Transformations: Politics, Economics and Culture,* Cambridge: Polity Press.

Hemmer, C. and Katzenstein, P. (2002). 'Why is There no NATO in Asia? Collective Identity, Regionalism and the Origins of Multilateralism', *International Organisation* 56 (3): 575–607.

Higgott, R. and Reich, S. (1998) *Globalization and Sites of Conflict: Towards Definition and Taxonomy*, CSGR Working Paper no. 01/98, Coventry: University of Warwick.

Hirst, P. and Thompson, G. (1999) *Globalisation in Question: The International Economy and the Possibilities of Governance*, second edition, Cambridge: Polity Press.

Hobbes, T. (1996) *Leviathan*, ed R. Tuck, Cambridge: Cambridge University Press.

Hooper, C. (2001) *Manly States: Masculinities, International Relations and Gender Politics*, New York: Columbia University Press.

Hutchings, K. (1999) *International Political Theory: Rethinking Ethics in a Global Era*, thousand Oaks, CA: Sage.

Jackson, R. (2000) *The Global Covenant: Human Conduct in a World of States*, Oxford: Oxford University Press.

Jackson, R. and Sørenson, G. (2003) *Introduction to International Relations: Theories and Approaches*, second edition, Oxford: Oxford University Press.

Janis, M.W. (1984) 'Jeremy Bentham and the Fashioning of "International Law"', *American Journal of International Law* 78 (2): 405–418.

Jensen, R. (2001) 'The United States, International Policing and the War again Anarchist Terrorism, 1900–1914', *Terrorism and Political Violence* 13 (1): 15–46.

Jervis, R. (1992) 'A Political Science Perspective on the Balance of Power and the Concert', *American Historical Review* 97 (3): 716–724.

Jervis, R. (1999) 'Realism, Neo-liberalism and Cooperation: Understanding the Debate', *International Security* 24 (1): 42–63.

Joekes, S. (1987) *Women in the World Economy: An INSTRAW Study*, New York: Oxford University Press.

Jones, R.J.B. (1981) 'The English School of International Relations: A Case for Closure', *Review of International Studies* 7 (1): 1–14.

Kant, I. (2002 [1785]) *Groundwork for the Metaphysics of Morals*, ed. T. Hill and A. Zweig, Oxford: Oxford University Press.

Kant, I. (1983 [1795]) *Perpetual Peace*, trans. T. Humphrey, Indianapolis, IN: Hackett.

Keene, E. (2005) *International Political Thought: A Historical Introduction*, Cambridge: Polity Press.

Kegley, C. (1993) 'The Neoidealist Moment? Realist myths and the New International Realities', *International Studies Quarterly* 37 (2): 131–147.

Keohane, R. (1988) 'International Institutions: Two Approaches', *International Studies Quarterly* 32 (4): 379–396.

Keohane, R. (1989a) *International Institutions and State Power: Essays in International Relations Theory*, Boulder, CO: Westview Press.

Keohane, R. (1989b) 'International Relations Theory: Contributions of a Feminist Standpoint', *Millennium* 18: 245–253.

Keohane, R. (1991) 'International Relations Theory: Contributions of a Feminist Standpoint', in R. Grant and K. Newland (eds) *Gender and International Relations*, Buckingham: Open University Press. Also available in *Millemium* 18 (1989): 245–253.

Keohane, R. (1998) 'Beyond Dichotomy: Conversations between International Relations and Feminist Theory', *International Studies Quarterly* 42: 193–198.

Keohane, R. and Nye, S. (1971) *Transnational Relations and World Politics*, Cambridge MA.: Harvard University Press.

Keohane, R. and Nye, J. (1977) *Power and Interdependence: World Politics in Transition*, Boston, MA: Little, Brown.

Klein, N. (2001) *No Logo*, London: Flamingo.

Krasner, R. (1995) 'Compromising Westphalia', *International Security* 20 (3): 115–151.

Lapid, Y. (1989) 'The Third Debate: On the Prospects of International Theory in a Post-Positivist Era', *International Studies Quarterly* 33: 235–254.

Levy, J.S. (1989) 'The Causes of War: a Review of Theories and Evidence', in P.E. Tetlock, J.L. Husbands, R. Jervis, P.C. Stern and C. Tilly (eds) *Behaviour, Society, and Nuclear War*, vol. 1, New York: Oxford University Press.

Linklater, A. (1998) *The Transformation of Political Community: Ethical Foundations of the Post-Westphalian Era*, Cambridge: Polity Press.

Locher, B. and Prügl, E. (2001) 'Feminism and Constructivism: Worlds Apart or Sharing the Middle Ground?' *International Studies Quarterly* 45 (1): 111–129.

Locke, J. (1988 [1688]) *Two Treatises of Government*, ed. P. Laslett, Cambridge: Cambridge University Press.

Machiavelli, N. (1988) *The Prince*, ed. Q. Skinner and R. Price, Cambridge: Cambridge University Press.

Marks, G. and Hooghe, L. (1996) 'European Integration and the State: Multi-level vs. State Centric Governance', *Journal of Common Market Studies* 34 (3): 341–378.

Marx, K. and Engels, F. (1992) *The Communist Manifesto*, Oxford: Oxford University Press.

Mearsheimer, J. (2001) *The Tragedy of Great Power Politics*, New York: W.W. Norton.

Mearsheimer, J. (2005) 'E.H. Carr vs. Idealism: The Battle Rages On', *International Relations* 19 (2): 139–152.

Mearsheimer, J. versus P. Rogers, R. Little, C. Hill, C. Brown and K. Booth (2005) 'Roundtable: the Battle Rages On', *International Relations* 19 (3): 337–361.

Merry, S.E. (2006) *Human Rights and Gender Violence: Translating International Law into Local Justice*, Chicago, IL: University of Chicago Press.

Morgenthau, H. (1985 [1948]) *Politics among Nations: The Pursuit of Power and Peace*, Chicago, IL: University of Chicago Press.

Munck, R. (2002) *Globalisation and Labour: The New 'Great Transformation'*, London: Zed Books.

Nabulsi, K. (1999) *Traditions of War: Occupation, Resistance, and the Law*, Oxford: Oxford University Press.

Narine, S. (2002) *Explaining ASEAN: Regionalism in Southeast Asia*, Boulder, CO: Lynne Rienner.

Newell, P. (2006) 'Climate for Change? Civil Society and the Politics of Global Warming', in M. Glasius, M. Kaldor and H. Anheier (eds) *Global Civil Society 2005/6*, London: Sage, pp. 90–119.

Nye, J. and Keohane, R. (1971) 'Transnational Relations and World Politics', *International Organization*, 25 (3): 329–349.

Ohmae, K. (1999) *The Borderless World: Power and Strategy in the Interlinked Economy*, revised edition, London: Collins.

O'Neill, O. (1991) 'Transnational Justice', in D. Held (ed.) *Political Theory Today*, Cambridge: Polity Press.

Oppenheim, L. (1955) *International Law: A Treatise*, London: Longmans Green.

Osiander, A. (2001) 'Sovereignty, International Relations and the Westphalian Myth', *International Organization* 55 (2): 251–287.

Østerud, Ø. (1996) 'Antinomies of Postmodernism in International Studies', *Journal of Peace Research* 33 (4): 385–390.

Overbeek, H. (2005) 'Global Governance, Class, Hegemony: A Historical Materialist Perspective', in A.D. Ba and M. Hoffman (eds) *Contending Perspectives on Global Governance*, London: Routledge, pp. 39–56.

Owen, J. (1994) 'How Liberalism Produces Democratic Peace', *International Security* 19 (2): 87–125.

Peterson, S. (2003) *A Critical Rewriting of Global Political Economy: Integrating Reproductive, Productive and Virtual Economies*, London: Routledge.

Peterson, V.S. and Runyan, A.S. (1999) *Global Gender Issues: Dilemmas in World Politics*, second edition, Boulder, Co: Westview Press.

Pettman, J. (1996) *Wording Women: A Feminist International Politics*, London: Routledge.

Pogge, T. (2002) *World Poverty and Human Rights: Cosmopolitan Responsibilities and Reforms*, Cambridge: Polity Press.

Polanyi, K. (1957) *The Great Transformation: The Political and Economic Origins of Our Time*, Boston, MA: Beacon Press.

Quataert, D. (2003) *The Ottoman Empire 1700–1922*, Cambridge: Cambridge University Press.

Quirk, J. and Vigneswaran, D. (2005) 'The Construction of an Edifice: The Story of the First Great Debate', *Review of International Studies* 31: 89–107.

Rai, S. (2002) *Gender and the Political Economy of Development*, Cambridge: Polity Press.

Raustiala, K. (1997) 'States, NGOs and International Environmental Institutions', *International Studies Quarterly* 41 (4): 719–7.

Raymond, G.A. (1998–1999) 'Necessity in Foreign Policy', *Political Science Quarterly* 113 (4): 673–688.

Razavi, S. (1999) 'Gendered Poverty and Well-being', *Development and Change* 30 (2): 409–434.

Reich, R. (1992) *The Work of Nations: Preparing Ourselves for 21st Century Capitalism*, New York: Vintage.

Rengger, N. (2002) 'On the Just War Tradition in the Twenty First Century', *International Affairs* 78 (2): 353–363.

Reus-Smit, C. (2005) 'Constructivism', in S. Burchill and A. Linklater *et al.* (eds) *Theories of International Relations*, third edition, Basingstoke: Palgrave MacMillan.

Risse-Kapen, T. (1995) *Bringing Transnational Relations Back In: Non-state Actors, Domestic Structures and International Institutions*, Cambridge: Cambridge University Press.

Roberts, A. and Guellf, R. (2000) *Documents on the Laws of War*, Oxford: Oxford University Press.

Rosamond, B. (2003) 'Babylon and On? Globalisation and International Political Economy', *Review of International Political Economy* 10 (4): 661–671.

Rosen, E. (2002) *Making Sweatshops: The Globalisation of the U.S. Apparel Industry*, Berkeley, CA: University of California Press.

Rosenau, J. (1995) 'Governance in the 21st Century', *Global Governance* 1 (1): 13–43.

Rosenberg, J. (2000) *The Follies of Globalisation Theory: Polemical Essays*, London: Verso.

Salamon, L.M. (1994) 'The Rise of the Non-Profit Sector', *Foreign Affairs* 73 (4): 109–122.

Salzinger, L. (2003) *Genders in Production: Making Workers in Mexico's Global Factories,* Berkeley, CA: University of California Press.

Schmidt, B.C. (1998) 'Lessons from the Past: Reassessing the Interwar Disciplinary History of International Relations', *International Studies Quarterly* 42 (3): 433–459.

Schmidt, B.C. (2004) 'Realism as Tragedy', *Review of International Studies* 30: 427–441.

Scholte, J.A. (2000) *Globalization: A Critical Introduction*, London: Macmillan.

Scholte, J.A. (2005) *Globalization: A Critical Introduction*, second edition, Basingstoke: Palgrave Macmillan.

Shearer, D. (1998) 'Outsourcing War', *Foreign Policy* 112: 68–81.

Sheehan, M. (1996) *The Balance of Power: History and Theory*, London: Routledge.

Singer, P. (1972) 'Famine, Affluence and Morality' *Philosophy and Public Affairs* 1 (1): 229–243.

Singer, P. (1979) *Practical Ethics*, Cambridge: Cambridge University Press.

Singer, P. (2002) *One World: The Ethics of Globalization*, New Haven, CT: Yale University Press.

Sklair, L. (2002) *Globalization: Capitalism and its Alternatives*, Oxford: Oxford University Press.

Smith, S. (1992) 'The Forty Years' Detour: The Resurgence of Normative Theory in International Relations', *Millennium: Journal of International Studies* 21: 490–514.

Smith, S. (1995) 'Self-Images of a Discipline: A Genealogy of International Relations Theory', in K. Booth and S. Smith (eds) *International Relations Theory Today*, Cambridge: Polity Press.

Smith, S. (1996) 'Positivism and Beyond', in S. Smith, K. Booth and M. Zalewski (EDS) *International Theory: Positivism and Beyond*, Cambridge: Cambridge University Press.

Smith, S. (1997) 'Epistemology, Postmodernism and International Relations Theory', *Journal of Peace Research* 34 (3): 330–336.

Smith, S. (2000) 'The Discipline of International Relations: Still an American Social Science?', *British Journal of Politics and International Relations* 2 (3): 374–402.

Spero, J. (1990) *The Politics of International Economic Relations*, fourth edition, London: Routledge.

Steans, J. (1998) *Gender and International Relations: An Introduction*, Cambridge: Polity Press.

Steans, J. (2003) 'Engaging from the Margins: Feminist Encounters with the "mainstream" of International Relations', *British Journal of Politics and International Relations* 5 (3): 428–454.

Sterling-Folker, J. (2000) 'Competing Paradigms or Birds of a Feather?' Constructivism and Neoliberal Institutionalism Compared', *International Studies Quarterly* 44 (1): 97–119.

Stevenson, N. (2000) 'Globalisation and Cultural Political Economy', in R. Germain (ed.) *Globalization and its Critics*, Basingstoke: Palgrave Macmillan, pp. 91–116.

Stopford, J. and Strange, S. (1991) *Rival States, Rival Firms: Competition for World Market Share*, Cambridge: Cambridge University Press.

Strange, S. (1994a) *States and Markets*, second edition, London: Pinter.

Strange, S. (1994b) 'Wake Up, Krasner, the World has Changed!', *Review of International Political Economy* 1 (2): 209–219.

Stubbs, R. (2004) 'ASEAN: Building Regional Co-operation', in M. Beeson (ed.) *Contemporary Southeast Asia: Regional Dynamics, National Differences*, Basingstoke: Palgrave MacMillan, pp. 216–233.

Stubbs, R. and Underhill, G. (eds) (2000) *Political Economy and the Changing Global Order*, second edition, Oxford: Oxford University Press.

Sutch, P. (2001) *Ethics, Justice and International Relations*, London: Routledge.

Teschke, B. and Heine, C. (2002) 'The Dialectic of Globalization: A Critique of Social Constructivism', in M. Rupert and H. Smith (eds.) *Historical Materialism and Globalization*, London: Routledge, pp. 165–187.

Thucydides (1972) *History of the Peloponnesian War*, trans. R. Warner, Harmondsworth: Penguin.

Tickner, J.A. (1997) 'You Just Don't Understand: Troubled Engagements between Feminists and IR Theorists', *International Studies Quarterly* 41 (4): 611–632.

Udombana, N. (2005) 'When Neutrality is a Sin: The Darfur Crisis and the Crisis of Humanitarian Intervention in Sudan', *Human Rights Quarterly* 27: 1149–1199.

UN (2005) *The Millennium Development Goals Report 2005*, New York, available at http://unstats.un.org/unsd/mi/pdf/MDG%20Book.pdf

UNDP (1994) *Human Development Report 1994: New Dimensions of Human Security*, Oxford: Oxford University Press, also available at http://hdr.undp.org/reports/global/1994/en/

UNDP (2002) *Human Development Report 2002: Deepening Democracy in a Fragmented World*, Oxford: Oxford University Press, also available at http://hdr.undp.org/reports/global/2002/en/

UNDP (2003) *Human Development Report 2003: Millennium Development Goals: A Compact Among Nations to End Human Poverty*, New York: Oxford University Press.

Vasquez, J. (1983) *The Power of Power Politics: A Critique*, New Brunswick, NJ: Rutgers University Press.

Vattel, E. (1916 [1758]) *The Law of Nations*, trans. C.G. Fenwick, Washington, DC: Carnegie Institution of Washington.

Viner, J. (1948) 'Power Versus Plenty in Objectives of Foreign Policy in the Seventeenth and Eighteenth Centuries', *World Politics*, 11 (1): 1–29.

Waever, O. (1996) 'The Rise and Fall of the Inter-Paradigm Debate', in S. Smith, K. Booth and M. Zalewski (eds) *International Theory: Positivism and Beyond*, Cambridge: Cambridge University Press.

Waever, P. (1998) 'The Sociology of a Not So International Discipline: American and European Developments in International Relations', *International Organization* 52 (4): 6878–727.

Waever, O. (2004) 'Isms, paradigms, traditions and theories – but why also "schools" in IR? A paper that gradually mutates into Prolegomena to a Posthumous Textbook: How should we teach (IR?) theory in a post-international age?', http://www.sgir.org/conference2004/papers/Waever%20-%20Isms.pdf, accessed January 2006.

Walker, T. and Morton, J. (2005) 'Re-Assessing the "Power of Power Politics" Thesis: Is Realism Still Dominant?', *International Studies Review* 7: 341–356.

Walt, S. (1998) 'International Relations: One World Many Theories', *Foreign Policy* 110: 29–46.

Waltz, K. (1959) *Man, the State and War: A Theoretical Analysis*, New York: Columbia University Press.

Waltz, K. (1979) *Theory of International Politics*, New York: McGraw-Hill.

Waltz, K. (2004) 'Neo-Realism: Confusions and Criticisms', *Journal of Politics and Society* 25: 1–6, Columbia University, http://www.coumbia.edu/cu/helvidius/files/2004-guest.pdf. (This article also forms the introduction to the new edition of *Theory of International Politics*.)

Walzer, M. (1978) *Just and Unjust Wars: A Moral Argument with Historical Illustrations*, New York: Basic Books.

Walzer, M. (2004) *Arguing about War*, New Haven, CT: Yale University Press.

Waters, M. (1995) *Globalisation*, London: Routledge.

Watson, A. (1992) *The Evolution of International Society: A Comparative Historical Analysis*, London: Routledge.

Weber, C. (2001) *International Relations Theory: A Critical Introduction*, London: Routledge.

Weiss, L. (1998) *The Myth of the Powerless State: Governing the Economy in a Global Era*, Cambridge: Polity Press.

Weiss, T., Forsythe, D. and Coate, R. (2004) *The United Nations and Changing World Politics*, fourth edition, Boulder, CO: Westview Press.

Weldes, J. (2001) 'Globalisation is Science Fiction', *Millennium: Journal of International Studies* 30 (3): 647–667.

Wendt, A. (1987) 'The Agent-Structure Problem in International Relations Theory', *International Organization*, 41 (3): 335–370.

Wendt, A. (1992) 'Anarchy is What States Make of It: the Social Construction of Power Politics', *International Organization* 46 (2): 391–426.

Wendt, A. (1994) 'Collective Identity Formation and the International State', *American Political Science Review* 88: 384–96.

Wheeler, N. (2000) *Saving Strangers: Humanitarian Intervention in International Society*, Oxford: Oxford University Press.

Wight, M. (1991) *International Theory: The Three Traditions*, ed. G. Wight and B. Porter, Leicester: Leicester University Press.

Wight, M. (1995) *Power Politics*, ed. H. Bull and C. Holbraad, Harmondsworth: Penguin.

Willetts, P. (2005) 'Transnational Actors and International Organisations in Global Politics' in J. Baylis and S. Smith (eds) *The Globalization of World Politics*, third edition, Oxford: Oxford University Press, pp. 425–450.

Williams, M. (1998) 'Identity and the Politics of Security', *European Journal of International Relations* 4 (2): 204–225.

Wilson, P. (1998) 'The Myth of the First Great Debate', *Review of International Studies* 24 (5): 1–15.

Woods, N. (2001) 'Making the IMF and World Bank more Accountable', *International Affairs*, Vol. 77, 1: 83–100.

Youngs, G. (2004) 'Feminist International Relations: A Contradiction in Terms? Or: Why Women and Gender are Essential to the World We Live in', *International Affairs* 80 (1): 75–87.

Yuval-Davis, N. and Anthias, F. (1989) *Women-Nation-State*, London: Macmillan.

Zehfuss, M. (2002) *Constructivism in International Relations: The Politics of Reality*, Cambridge: Cambridge University Press.

INDEX

intervention 167; intellectual history of 44–6; international/domestic politics distinction 106; international organizations 87–8; international political economy 134; Machiavelli 25–6; offensive 53; pessimism 68; as problem solving theory 116; rejection of morality 65; structural 46, 49–53, 58, 60, 187; war 161, 162, 163; *see also* neo-realism
reductionist theories 50–1
reflectivism 12, 13, 14, 114
Reformation 25, 26
regimes 102, 187, 189
regionalism 88–9, 90–1, 184, 189–90
Renaissance 25–6
Reus-Smit, C. 128
Rosamond, B. 149
Rosenberg, J. 132, 150
Runyan, Ann Sisson 122, 185
Rwanda 164, 167

Scholte, Jan Aart 143, 173–4, 176, 177
Seattle protests 152
Second World War 8, 55
security 16, 61, 158; competition 52, 53; human 163, 168–9, 174, 176–7; League of Nations 34; regional organizations 89, 90; security dilemma 43, 45, 190; social constructivism 126; *see also* collective security; war
self-determination 22–3, 85
Sheehan, Michael 30
Singer, Peter 76–7
Sklair, Leslie 141
Smith, Adam 133
Smith, Steve 14, 114, 115
social constructivism 14, 15, 62, 125–9, 182, 190; globalization

148; humanitarian intervention 169; regional security 89
social movements 93–4
social structures 50
solidarism 79, 168, 169, 170
Somalia 164, 167
sovereign states 4, 14–15, 31–2, 74, 160; English school 182; feminism 124; history of international relations 6, 22–3; public international law 189; realism 60–1, 109, 110; social constructivism 127; Waltz 51–2; *see also* states
sovereignty 4, 22–3, 56, 99, 104, 158; ASEAN 91; definition of 190; global economic justice 174, 175, 177; humanitarian intervention 17, 164, 165–6, 167–8, 170, 184; multilevel governance 88–9; Westphalian system 24, 27, 28, 191
Soviet Union (USSR), former 55–6, 57, 61, 112, 142
St Augustine 161
St Thomas Aquinas 161
state of nature 45, 66, 68, 69
statecraft 29, 33, 43
states 33, 75, 83, 102–3, 105–6, 160; globalization 133–4, 143–4, 145–7, 148; male dominance 124; new medievalism 103–4; realism 43, 48–9, 51–2; social constructivism 126–7; terrorism 98; *see also* sovereign states
Steans, Jill 123–4, 125
Stopford, J. 95
Strange, Susan 95, 133, 146, 184
structure 50, 51, 60, 127
Sudan 166–8
territoriality 24
terrorism 13, 16, 97–8, 103
textual analysis 121, 123
theory 4, 113, 115–16, 120